AF413519

INSTANT POT INDIAN VEGAN COOKBOOK

INSTANT POT
INDIAN VEGAN
COOKBOOK

UMA RAGHUPATHI

CONTENTS

ABOUT THE AUTHOR

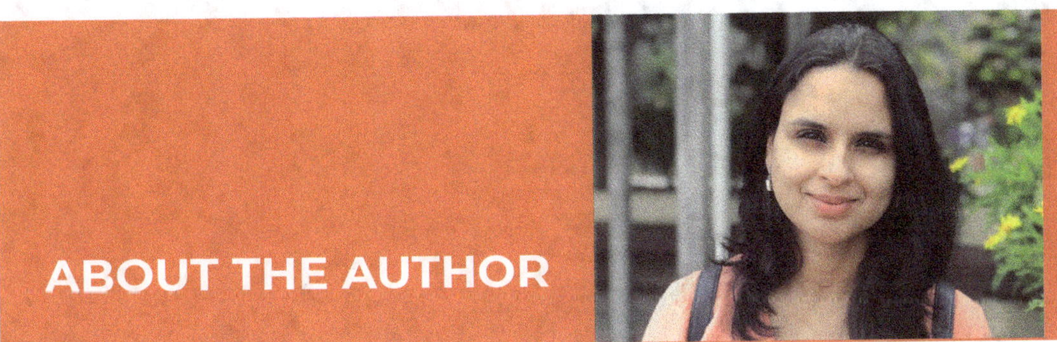

Uma Raghupathi has always been drawn to food and cooking. As she completed her law degree in India, she still made time to learn the basics of cooking common Indian medicinal and herbal foods. Fast forward fifteen years, and she is now the proud owner of *Simple Sumptuous Cooking*, a blog that brings together the flavors of diverse cuisines and spreads the joy of cooking. *Simple Sumptuous Cooking* has been featured in *Bloglovin', Flipboard, Foodgawker, Parade, and BuzzFeed*, among others. What started as a simple way to share time-saving and healthy recipes gathered momentum over the years, and Uma found her calling to write this book that she hopes will help millions discover the joy of cooking.

Uma lives in San Diego with her husband and two daughters. You can catch her writing from the comfort of her egg chair on her patio with a hot cup of chai.

INTRODUCTION

This book is about succeeding in the kitchen, not just getting by or managing to put a meal together at the last minute. The fact that you are reading this shows me you have a desire to prepare quality meals that will wow your family and friends.

First, let me assure you that your goal is a very worthy one, and second, you are not alone in this. The reason I compiled the recipes in the *Vegan Indian Instant Pot Cookbook* is to help fellow kitchen adventurers like myself have fun cooking in the most efficient way possible.

Lastly, let me congratulate you for choosing this book to take you there. If you follow the tips and techniques within these pages, I guarantee you will be as comfortable hosting a party or preparing a sumptuous meal as you are right now reading this book.

Why Motivate?

When I first began to cook for my family as a young adult, I felt myself being dragged into a predicament that most people are—cooking as a chore rather than as a conscious way to prepare a healthy meal for our loved ones. As I honed my cooking skills, I also strived to make the experiences memorable by staying true to the core purpose— to prepare simple, sumptuous, and sustainable meals. What is often missing for many of us is the simple reminder that some of the things we do may seem mundane, but they are more important than we realize. It is my intention to spark that motivation within you.

Why Instant Pot?

Most of us don't intend to be so busy that we barely have time to cook a quality meal for our family, yet that is exactly what happens a lot of the time. It is no surprise that the Instant Pot has revolutionized the way we plan and cook. I have tested this kitchen gadget to its extreme capacity, and I have a lot of do's and don'ts to share with you. There is even a Tips and Tricks section dedicated to this.

Why Vegan?

Cooking has been an adventure for me, and it has helped me develop a special relationship with food. When we pay attention to what we eat and where it came from, it takes very little time to discover that there is a lot of animal cruelty in food. So, I have changed my eating habits to be completely animal-free. Likewise, the recipes that I share on my blog and in this book reflect vegan principles. If you have not had any exposure to vegan cooking, my hope is that this book will convince you to join my family and me in fostering veganism.

How to Use This Book

In addition to the recipes, I want this book to be a quick reference for you in your kitchen, so I have included lots of tips and tricks, common measurement references, and a little background on all the spices common to Indian cuisine that you can keep as a handy reference.

ESSENTIAL ELEMENTS OF INDIAN COOKING

Indian cooking is all about spices. You get the right spice mix for the right kind of dish, and you are more than halfway there! So, let's get to the basics about spices and other ingredients you will come across as you perfect your culinary skills.

There are some favorites and some that are not so popular, but they are equally important nonetheless. I have used a variety of spices in my dishes, some of which you may have never heard of. But not to worry, you will not only become familiar with them, but you will also learn to use them in the right proportions for the right dish soon enough.

Cumin Seeds

Cumin seeds are known for their distinctive aroma and flavor. They add earthy character to food, and hence it is a staple in stews, soups, curries, chutneys, biryanis, etc. Loaded with antioxidants, cumin seeds have a special place in Indian cuisine.

Garam Masala

Garam masala translates to a hot mixture of spices. It is the most popular spice mixture that you would typically need for most curries. Although widely available in stores, garam masala can also be prepared at home for a fraction of the cost and with better flavor. Some of the key ingredients in garam masala are fennel, bay leaves, black and white peppercorns, cloves, cinnamon, mace, cardamom, cumin, coriander seeds, and red chili powder. Most Indian recipes that are prepared with an onion/garlic base need garam masala.

Bay Leaves

Bay leaves have a mildly pungent yet sharp and bitter taste if eaten whole. They are more known for their fragrance than taste, as is typical of most spices. It is one of several ingredients in garam masala and is used in rice dishes like biryani. Bay leaves are at their best when crushed or ground before cooking for most dishes, and they can also be used whole for a few dishes.

Cardamom

Cardamom is a spice used mainly for its flavor and aroma. A couple of pods of cardamom seeds go a long way in adding a ton of flavor, so it is a good option to add in rice dishes and also in drinks like masala chai.

Asafoetida

Likely the most underrated condiment in Indian cuisine, asafoetida does not add to the taste and has a mild flavor. The primary benefit of asafoetida is how it aids digestion. It is commonly used along with turmeric, and it is a standard component of lentil curries such as dal, as well as vegetable dishes with potatoes and cauliflower.

Mustard Seeds

This is a must-have spice in any Indian kitchen. Almost all curries in south Indian cuisine need mustard seeds during the tempering step, wherein they are sautéed in a teaspoon of oil until they sputter and release the flavors into the curry.

Red Chili Powder

Red chili powder is yet another commonly available ingredient. Chilies come in various spice levels and flavors. For dishes that need flavor more than heat, Kashmiri red chili powder suits best, while the opposite is the case for Byadagi chilies.

Coriander Powder

Coriander powder, made from toasted and ground coriander seeds, has a lemony flavor and is used either in its raw form or in the tempering process.

Cumin Powder

Cumin powder, made from toasted and ground cumin seeds, is a great flavor addition to any dish when used in moderation. Since it has a calming effect on our body, it is generally used in spicy dishes to balance the nutrition and palate.

Mango Powder

As the name suggests, mango powder is the fruity spice powder made from dried, unripe green mangoes. Also known commercially as amchur, it is used as a seasoning spice to add a tangy flavor in dishes like samosa and pakora. It can also be used in fruit salads, curries, and chutneys.

Black Pepper

Black pepper is a key spice found in cuisines all over the world. It plays a special role in Indian cuisine too. Dishes that are otherwise bland get a flavor boost with black pepper.

Other Pantry Staples

Apart from the spices listed above, there are other indispensable pantry supplies you will need to get the most out of this book. While it's not practical to call out each of them, the important ones are listed below.

Lentils

I use varieties of lentils like pigeon pea (toor dal), red lentils (masoor dal), brown lentils, mung bean (moong dal), black lentils (urad dal), and yellow split peas (chana dal).
Store these in an air-tight container for extended shelf life.

Beans

Some of the common beans that are good to have in your pantry for Indian cooking are red kidney beans, chickpeas, black beans, and black-eyed peas.

P.S.: It's a lot cheaper and healthier to buy dried beans instead of the canned type.

Rice and Millets

Rice and millets come in a dozen varieties, each with its own texture and cooking method. Using the appropriate water ratio is a key step to getting the proper texture. New crops generally tend to require less water to cook and vice versa.

Basmati rice fits the bill for most recipes that need long strands of grains that don't stick to each other. Other commonly used rice varieties are sona masoori and jasmine rice.

Millets are a great substitute for rice and also come in a variety of kinds. They are generally more forgiving in texture sensitivity compared to rice.

Non-Dairy Milk

There are varieties of non-dairy milk, so you can choose your favorites. I use almond milk, oat milk, and coconut milk more frequently than any other kind, and I prefer going with unsweetened almond milk or oat milk for my curries, chai, and vegan desserts.

Canned coconut milk or cream is a great way to add richness to a dish. I often use canned coconut milk for dishes like eggplant curry and lentil curry, and they have always turned out great! I always keep several cans of coconut milk stocked up in my pantry.

Nuts

Indians tend to include toasted nuts in rice and curry dishes, as well as desserts. I mostly use cashews and almonds in my recipes. Cashew nuts also come in handy as a thickener to replace heavy cream for vegan dishes.

Oils

Some of the common options for cooking oils are coconut oil, olive oil, corn oil, avocado oil, and sesame oil. Coconut oil is generally a good fit for most Indian dishes. If you are not a big fan of the aroma or flavor of coconut oil, use corn oil or olive oil.

Frozen Pantries

Although fresh ingredients are a better bet, sometimes it's just not practical. A case in point is frozen coconuts! Grated coconuts are indispensable for south Indian cuisine. Frozen grated coconuts are a godsend for such dishes. With a little bit of thawing time, they blend very well with spices.

Frozen Fruits and Vegetables

Frozen fruits and vegetables come to the rescue for seasonal dishes. Frozen peas, corn, and mango spears come in handy for preparing certain special dishes any time of the year.

MY GO-TO KITCHEN TOOLS

The right tools and gadgets make all the difference in preparing a hearty meal in a short time. Since this book is all about the Instant Pot, we are not talking about any other special gadget.

A few of the basics you will need are:

- handled trivet
- hand blender
- ginger grater
- pestle
- extra silicone rings
- sharp knives
- cutting board
- extra inner pot for Instant Pot
- small steel pots that fit inside the inner pot
- coffee grinder (to grind a small batch of spices)

INSTANT POT TIPS AND TRICKS

Cooking can be a long and tedious task for the unprepared soul. That's why the Instant Pot is such a blessing. This electric pressure cooker does everything for you! Here are some tips to help you get the best results from your Instant Pot.

- As you prepare to boil or pressure cook anything in the Instant Pot, be sure to fill up the inner pot at least halfway, but not more than two-thirds. Filling it up more can prevent natural pressure from building inside the pot and can cause an unsafe condition.
- It is always better to soak the rice and beans if your recipe calls for these ingredients. Soaking speeds up the cooking process with an Instant Pot.
- Always sauté in medium mode to keep your curry from burning before you can make adjustments.
- Just before the step of adding water for curries, scrape the inner pot to release the flavors, then give it a good stir before closing the lid.
- If you are preparing a dessert, wash your silicone ring and lid with warm soapy water to get rid of any residual odors.
- Avoid dry roasting spices inside the inner pot to prolong the life and look of your Instant Pot. Instead, use oil or water to sauté the spices and veggies.
- Clean your Instant Pot at least twice a week with a warm wet cotton towel to keep it looking great and to extend its life.

MEASUREMENT AND CONVERSIONS

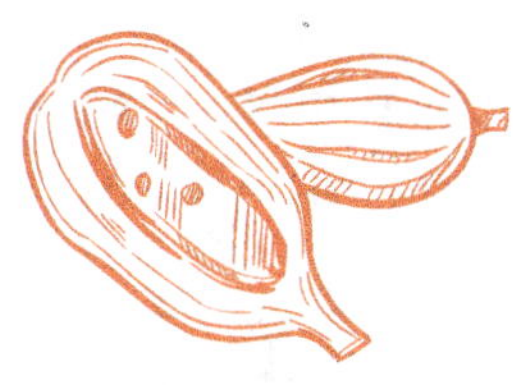

When it comes to Instant Pot cooking, the timer setting is too important a detail to overlook. But the challenge is remembering the time required for the key ingredients. A few minutes too much or too little can mean a lot for the texture and taste of your dish. Use the chart below as a quick reference for cooking time for basic ingredients you will come across in this book.

Grain	Water Ratio (cups of water)	Cooking Time (mins.)
Pearl barley	1:2.5	20-22
Couscous	1:2	2-3
Millet	1:1.75	10-12
Rolled oats	1:2	2-3
Steel cut oats	1:3	3-5
Quinoa (quick cooking)	1:1.25	1
Rice (white, jasmine, and basmati)	1:1	4
Brown rice	1:1	20-22
Wild rice	1:2	20-25
Sorghum	1:3	20-25

Given the variety of beans and legumes available, they need a chart of their own. Moreover, a little prep work by soaking the beans for three to four hours before using them is a huge time saver, as you will notice from the chart below.

Beans, Legumes, and Lentils	Cooking Time (dry)	Cooking Time (pre-soaked)
Black beans	20-25	6-8
Black-eyed peas	14-18	4-5
Chickpeas	35-40	10-15
Cannellini beans	30-35	6-9
Red kidney beans	15-20	7-8
Lentils (green)	8-10	6
Lentils (brown)	8-10	6
Lentils (red, split)	6	4
Lentils (yellow, split moong dal)	6	4
Lima beans	12-14	6-10
Navy beans	20-25	7-8
Pinto beans	25-30	6-9
Peas	16-20	10-12
Soybeans	35-45	18-20

Below are some commonly used measurements in this book that could come in handy when you are trying out the recipes.

Unit	Other Equivalent	Weight Equivalent
1 teaspoon	⅓ tablespoon	⅙ fl. ounces
1 tablespoon	3 teaspoons	½ fl. ounces
⅛ cup	2 tablespoons	1 fl. ounce
¼ cup	4 tablespoons	2 fl. ounces
⅓ cup	¼ cup + 4 tbsp.	2 ¾ fl. ounces
½ cup	8 tablespoons	4 fl. ounces
1 cup	½ pint	8 fl. ounces
1 pint	2 cups	16 fl. ounces
1 quart	4 cups	32 fl. ounces
1 liter	1 quart + ¼ cup	4 ¼ cups
1 gallon	4 quarts	16 cups

INSTANT POT Q&A'S

I have noticed from my blog that there are a lot of people who are not yet comfortable using the Instant Pot. Perhaps you had a bad experience once or twice, or you are not familiar with pressure cooking, but don't let that stop you from missing out on this huge time saver. A couple of minutiae is all it takes to make or break a great dish. Here are some common questions and answers that dispel any doubts about using an Instant Pot for vegan Indian cuisine.

Is an Instant Pot a good fit for vegans?

With multi-functional settings for slow cooking, pressure cooking, steaming, sautéing, and baking, the Instant Pot caters to all cuisines. For Indian dishes, you would be primarily using the pressure-cooking setting more than others.

Why is my pot spitting steam?

If the lid is not on properly or if the seal is not properly placed, steam tends to release, and it appears as if it is spitting, sometimes with tiny water droplets too. However, it is common to see some steam coming from the valve until it floats up and seals.

Can I leave my Instant Pot unattended?

Yes, you can leave it unattended while it cooks on a preset timer. You also have an option to keep it warm after it stops cooking. This works out very well if you are running errands while the Instant Pot does the work for you. Keep in mind that leaving electrical appliances plugged in overnight is not recommended.

Does an Instant Pot heat up the house?

Unlike the electric range or the oven, the Instant Pot does not add a noticeable load on your air conditioning system! This makes a huge difference, especially in the summertime.

Why do I get a burn sign?

These are the common reasons you can get burn signs in your inner pot:

- not enough water/liquid
- spices staying in the bottom
- scalding of certain dairy products such as cream or milk

To avoid these common issues, be sure to add enough liquid and mix well before closing the lid.

How do I clean my Instant Pot?

With the Instant Pot unplugged, use a cotton rag with warm soapy water to wipe the exterior and interior. Always make sure there are no water drops making their way inside the cooker.

How do I get rid of the odor from the sealing ring?

With a few easy steps, you can prevent the rubbery odor from the sealing ring.

- Remove and wash the sealing ring after each use. Having a spare sealing ring means you will have one ready to use all the time.

- As you stow away the Instant Pot after each use, flip over the lid and place it on the top of the pot. This way, the sealing ring is well ventilated at all times.
- Keep a sealing ring for savory dishes and one for desserts. This way the food flavors are not mixed up.

What does NPR mean?

NPR stands for natural pressure release, which is a common cooking method for Indian recipes. If a recipe calls for NPR, let the pot cool down naturally after the timer expires and until the pin resets. The other way to release pressure is by using the quick release option, if the recipe calls for that.

RECIPES

Instant Pot Soups

We've all been there. After a long day at work, you don't feel like cooking a meal. Or it's too cold or too hot to lift your spirits and spend a lot of time in the kitchen. Now is the time to take out your handy dandy electric pressure cooker: the Instant Pot!

Let's explore some soup recipes that can be easily prepared with the Instant Pot.

KALE LENTIL SOUP

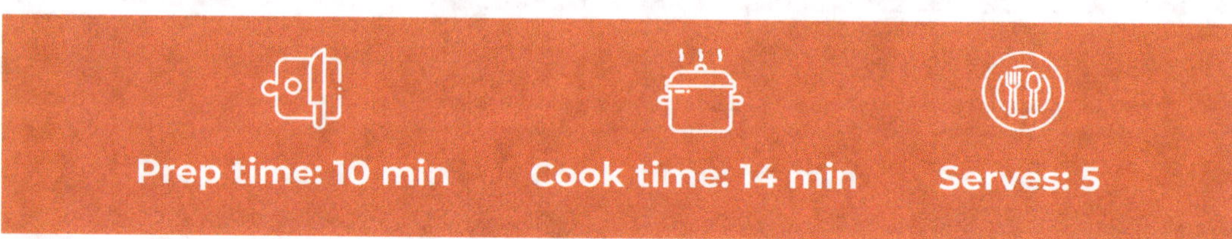

INGREDIENTS

1 ½ cups lentils
(use brown or green lentils)
2 ½ cups kale leaves, chopped
2 large carrots, chopped
3 Roma tomatoes, chopped
1 teaspoon red chili powder
½ - 1 teaspoon black pepper
¼ teaspoon turmeric powder
1 teaspoon cumin powder
2 cloves garlic, minced
½ inch ginger, grated
2 bay leaves
2 small cinnamon sticks
4 cloves (Indian spice)
pink salt, 1 - 2 teaspoons
½ teaspoon thyme (optional)
3 cups organic vegetable broth
1½ - 2 cups water
2 tablespoons chives (optional)
1 medium onion, chopped
2 tablespoons olive oil

INSTRUCTIONS

1. Drizzle oil into inner pot. Press 'sauté' and when the oil is hot, add bay leaves, cinnamon, and cloves.
2. Follow up with ginger and garlic. Stir constantly for a minute or until the garlic turns golden brown.
3. Add onions and stir constantly for 1 minute.
4. Add kale and continue to cook for 30 seconds.
5. Add carrots and tomatoes.
6. Add all the spices and stir for 1 minute.
7. Add lentils, vegetable broth, water, salt, and thyme. Stir for about 30 seconds.
8. Close lid. Turn 'steam release' handle to 'sealing' position. Press 'pressure cook' and set time for 10 minutes.
9. When time is up, open lid using the 'quick release' button.

POTATO CORN CHOWDER

 **Prep time: 10 min**    **Cook time: 8 min**    **Serves: 4**

INGREDIENTS

4 red potatoes, cubed

1 cup frozen corn kernels or fresh corn

½ cup carrots, chopped

½ cup coconut cream

4 cups organic vegetable broth/ stock

2 cloves garlic, minced

1 onion, diced

½ teaspoon red chili powder or cayenne pepper

½ teaspoon black pepper powder

½ teaspoon Italian seasoning

2 tablespoons cornstarch

1 tablespoon olive oil

INSTRUCTIONS

1. Press 'sauté' and add a couple of teaspoons of oil.
2. As the oil heats up, add minced garlic cloves and chopped onions.
3. Sauté for 2 to 3 minutes, stirring regularly until they turn light brown in color.
4. Add potatoes, frozen corn, chopped carrots, coconut cream, Italian seasoning, salt and pepper, and vegetable stock. Stir well. Press 'cancel.'
5. Close lid and turn valve from 'venting' to 'sealing' position.
6. Set to 'manual/pressure cook' (high pressure) and set the timer to 8 minutes.
7. Wait for 'natural pressure release' (NPR) when the silver button on lid drops.
8. Meanwhile, mix the cornstarch with 3 tablespoons of water.
9. Add cornstarch mixture and cayenne powder and press sauté. Cook for 1 minute, then switch off heat.
10. Let simmer for 10 minutes.
11. Garnish with fresh chopped parsley and serve hot!

CABBAGE SOUP

Prep time: 10 min   **Cook time: 20 min**   **Serves: 4 to 6**

INGREDIENTS:

2 teaspoons olive oil
1 teaspoon Italian seasoning
½ teaspoon black pepper
1 bay leaf
½ teaspoon dried sage
3 cups coarsely chopped green cabbage
2 cups vegetable broth
1 (14.5 ounces) can diced tomatoes
2 carrots, chopped
1 onion, chopped
2 garlic cloves, chopped
3 teaspoons lemon juice

INSTRUCTIONS

1. Press 'sauté' and add oil. When oil heats up, add chopped garlic and onions. Sauté for 1 minute. Add all ingredients one by one; give it a nice stir. Close and lock lid.
2. Press 'pressure cook' and set a timer to 7 minutes. Allow 10 minutes for pressure to build. Release pressure using natural release method.
3. Enjoy the cabbage soup!

PUMPKIN SOUP

This fall-flavored pumpkin soup is made without heavy cream. Enjoy with your favorite toppings.

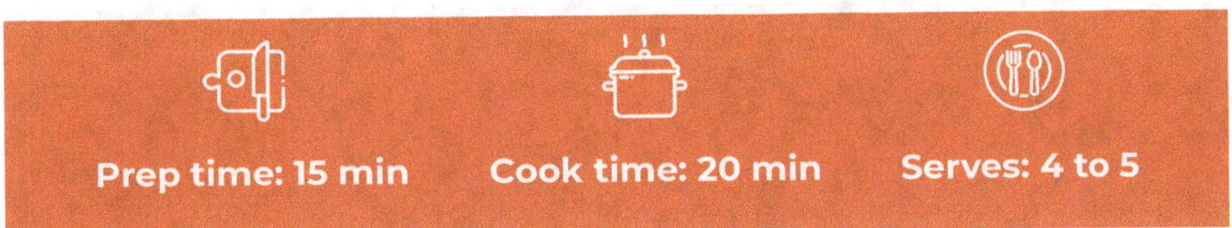

INGREDIENTS

4 cups peeled fresh pumpkin, cubed

1 onion, chopped

2 teaspoons ginger, grated

4 garlic cloves, chopped

½ teaspoon black pepper

3 teaspoons olive oil

salt to taste

½ teaspoon red chili powder

3 cups vegetable broth

lemon juice

INSTRUCTIONS

1. Press 'sauté' and add oil to inner pot. When oil heats up, add grated ginger, chopped garlic, and chopped onion. Sauté until onion turns soft.
2. Add salt, black pepper, cubed and peeled pumpkin, and red chili powder. Sauté for 20 seconds.
3. Add vegetable broth, cover with lid, and turn to 'manual.' Turn lid valve to 'seal,' and set to high pressure for 10 minutes.
4. Release valve with a towel (be careful of the pressurized steam) and release steam until it stops. Open lid. Using a hand mixer, blend ingredients into a creamy soup. (If you don't have a hand blender, puree in a blender in batches once slightly cooled.)
5. Add lemon juice and serve soup with your favorite toppings.

CARROT GINGER SOUP

This is one of the easiest and creamiest Instant Pot soups. Perfect on wintery days!

INGREDIENTS

2 teaspoons coconut oil
1 onion, chopped
2 garlic cloves, grated
2 tablespoons ginger, grated
4 ½ cups carrots, peeled and chopped (7 to 8 carrots)
3 cups vegetable broth
½ teaspoon turmeric
½ teaspoon black pepper
salt to taste

INSTRUCTIONS

1. Press 'sauté' and add oil. Let pot heat up for a minute.
2. Add onion and stir frequently for 2 minutes or until onions have softened.
3. Add ginger and garlic, and stir frequently for 1 minute. Turn off the sauté function.
4. Add carrots, broth, turmeric, salt, and pepper, and give it a quick stir.
5. Close lid. Set the pressure valve to 'sealing' position and press 'manual/pressure cook.' Cook for 5 minutes on high pressure. Let the pressure release naturally for 5 minutes, and then do a quick pressure release.
6. Open lid. Puree cooked carrots using an immersion blender until smooth. (Make sure you remove all the big lumps.)
7. Enjoy this soup with your favorite toppings.

TOMATO SOUP

This delicious Instant Pot tomato soup is made with fresh herbs and veggies.

INGREDIENTS

4 large tomatoes, diced (about 3 cups)

1 onion, chopped

½ cup carrots, chopped

3 cloves garlic, minced

3 teaspoons olive oil

1 bay leaf

2 tablespoons fresh basil, chopped

salt to taste

½ teaspoon black pepper

2 cups vegetable stock

¼ cup coconut milk (optional)

INSTRUCTION

1. Press 'sauté.' Add oil and once it's hot, add bay leaf and minced garlic. Sauté for 30 seconds.
2. Add onions and sauté until they soften.
3. Add diced carrot, chopped tomatoes, vegetable stock, black pepper, and salt.
4. Close lid and turn pressure valve to 'sealing'. Set pot to 'manual/pressure cook' on high pressure and set timer to 5 minutes.
5. When the Instant Pot beeps, let the pressure release naturally. Open lid.
6. Remove bay leaf and puree the soup using a hand blender until smooth. (If you don't have a hand blender, puree in a blender in batches once slightly cooled.)
7. Add freshly chopped basil leaves and coconut milk.
8. Serve hot and top with croutons.

Instant Pot Rice Dishes

Nothing comes close to the heart of Indian cuisine as rice recipes do. Check out these easy Instant Pot dishes that you can prepare to entertain your guests. Happy cooking!

GARLIC RICE

Garlic rice is simple yet flavorful. You can use this as a side or main dish.

INGREDIENTS

2 cups basmati rice
2 garlic heads or 20 garlic
    cloves, chopped
2 teaspoons olive oil
¼ teaspoon turmeric powder
salt to taste
1 teaspoon mustard seeds
½ teaspoon urad dal

INSTRUCTIONS

1. Press 'sauté' on the Instant Pot, and add 2 teaspoons of oil, along with mustard seeds and urad dal. Sauté them until they turn golden.
2. Add chopped garlic, and continue to sauté until the garlic turns brown.
3. Add the rinsed rice, turmeric powder, salt, and 2 ¼ cups of water. Press 'cancel' and stir well.
4. Close the lid, press the 'pressure cook' setting, and set the timer for 4 minutes on high pressure.
5. Once the timer goes off, do a natural release, then remove lid.
6. Fluff rice with a fork. Instant Pot garlic rice is ready to be served hot!

TOMATO RICE

Tomato rice is delicious and flavorful. It is a perfect dish for lunch boxes.

Prep time: 8 min   Cook time: 20 min   Serves: 3

INGREDIENTS

1 cup sona masoori rice
2 ½ cups water
1 cup tomatoes, chopped
1 small onion, diced
3 teaspoons oil
½ teaspoon red chili powder
½ teaspoon cumin powder
1 teaspoon coriander powder
salt to taste
2 tablespoons cilantro for
   garnish

INSTRUCTIONS

1. Wash and rinse sona masoori rice, then put it aside.
2. Press 'sauté' and add oil. When oil is hot, add dry spice powder one by one. Sauté on low heat mode for thirty seconds.
3. Add chopped onions and tomatoes. Sauté until onion is translucent.
4. Add salt, rinsed rice, and water. Give a nice stir.
5. Put on lid and close 'pressure release' valve. Adjust to 'pressure cook' on high for 7 minutes.
6. Let the pressure release for 10 minutes naturally, then do a quick release. Open lid after pressure is released.
7. Garnish with cilantro. Fluff the rice with a fork. Tomato rice is ready to enjoy.

LEMON RICE

This lemon rice dish is easy to prepare and perfect for a lunch box. It is made with simple ingredients and sona masoori rice. Optionally, you can make it with basmati or jasmine rice. Make sure to adjust the water rice ratio accordingly.

INGREDIENTS

1 cup sona masoori rice
¼ cup peanuts, whole (optional)
1 teaspoon mustard seeds
1/2 teaspoon cumin seeds
1 dry red chili, whole
2 green chilies, chopped
1 tablespoon coconut oil
2 teaspoons ginger, grated
2 teaspoons turmeric root, grated or ¼ teaspoon turmeric powder
1 strand curry leaves
3 teaspoon lemon juice
salt to taste
2 tablespoons cilantro for garnishing (optional)

INSTRUCTIONS

1. Wash and rinse sona masoori rice, then put aside.
2. Add oil to inner pot, then press 'sauté.' When oil heats up, add peanuts, mustard seeds, cumin seeds, and red chili. Sauté for 1 minute or until peanuts are roasted.
3. Add grated ginger, turmeric, and curry leaves. Sauté for 20 seconds. Press 'cancel.' (sauté process)
4. Add drained rice, 2 ½ cups water, and salt. Give a nice stir.
5. Close lid and pressure-release valve. Adjust to 'pressure cook' on high for 8 minutes.
6. Let the pressure release for 10 minutes naturally, then do a quick release. Open lid after pressure is released.
7. Add lemon juice and garnish with cilantro (if desired). Fluff rice with a fork. Lemon rice is ready to enjoy.

MUSHROOM RICE

This is one recipe that truly is as easy to prepare as it sounds. With all the right spices in hand, you will be done with the cooking part in less than 30 minutes.

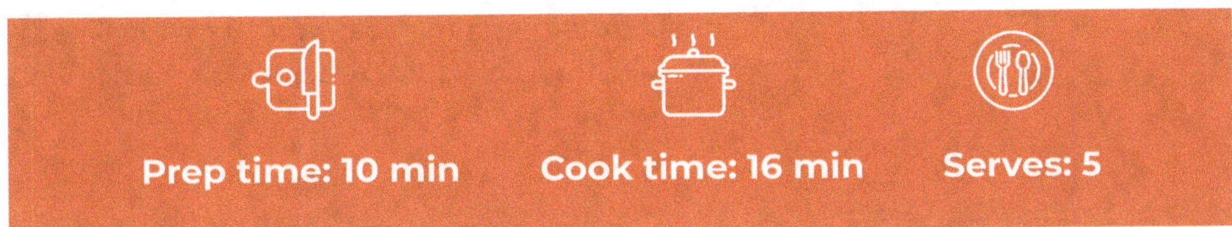

INGREDIENTS

2 tablespoons olive oil
2 tablespoons cashews, chopped (optional)
½ teaspoon cumin seeds/jeera
1 small bay leaf
2 green cardamoms, crushed
4 cloves (spice)
½ inch cinnamon stick
1 green chili, chopped
½ inch ginger, minced
2 garlic cloves, whole
1 medium-sized onion, chopped
½ teaspoon turmeric powder
1 teaspoon red chili powder (medium spice level)
½ teaspoon garam masala
salt to taste
8 ounces mushrooms, sliced
¼ cup coconut milk
1 cup basmati rice
1¼ cups water
1 tablespoon chopped cilantro for garnish (optional)

INSTRUCTIONS

1. Rinse rice and soak for at least 10 minutes.
2. Add oil to inner pot and press 'sauté.' When oil heats up, add cashews. Sauté for 1 minute. Please note adding cashews is optional but recommended.
3. Add jeera/cumin seeds, bay leaves, cloves, cardamom, and cinnamon, stirring constantly for 1 minute.
4. Add chopped ginger, chopped garlic, and chopped green chilies. Continue to sauté for 1 minute.
5. Add onions and cook for 1 to 2 minutes or until translucent.

6. Add garam masala, chili powder, and turmeric powder. Mix well.
7. Add sliced mushrooms and coconut milk, and stir continually for about 30 seconds.
8. Add salt, soaked rice, and water. Mix well.
9. Press 'cancel.' Close lid and pressure-release valve. Adjust to 'pressure cook' on high for 5 minutes.
10. Let the pressure release for 10 minutes naturally, then do a quick release. Fluff the rice with a fork.

VEGETABLE RICE

This is an easy one-pot rice dish mixed with a variety of vegetables and flavored with aromatic spices. I am sharing an easy way to cook this delicacy in less than 30 minutes.

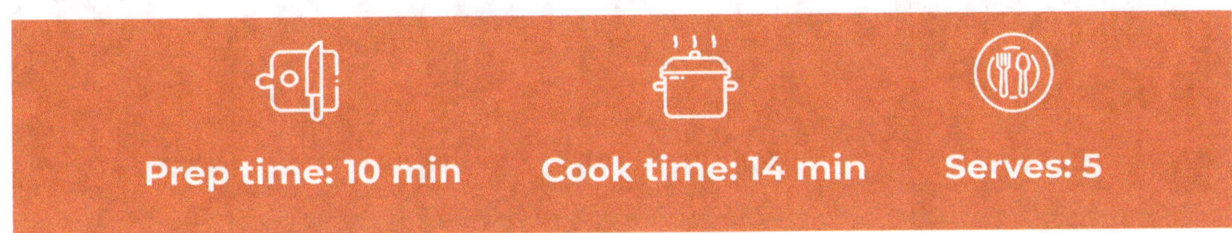

INGREDIENTS

2 cups basmati rice

2 ¼ cups water

1 cup green beans

2 carrots, chopped

1 cup red onions, chopped

1 garlic clove, chopped

½ inch ginger, grated

salt to taste

1 teaspoon ground coriander

1 teaspoon cumin powder

½ teaspoon red chili powder or Kashmiri red chili powder

2 cloves (spice), powdered

½ teaspoon black pepper powder

½ teaspoon cinnamon powder

1 tablespoon organic tomato paste or 1 tomato, chopped

5 to 8 tablespoons cashew paste or coconut cream

INSTRUCTIONS

1. Drizzle oil in inner pot. Press 'sauté.' When oil is hot, sauté ginger and garlic for about 1 minute with constant stirring.

2. Add onions and continue to cook for 1 more minute.

3. Add all the spices listed above and continue to stir.

4. Add tomato paste or fresh chopped tomatoes, carrots, and green beans. Stir well for 1 to 2 minutes.

5. Add cashew paste or coconut milk cream. Stir well.

6. Add rice and water as listed in the ingredients list and stir well to get an even mix.

7. Close the lid and turn the steam release handle to 'sealing' position. Press 'pressure cook' and set time for 4 minutes. When time is up, open lid using 10 minute natural release.

8. At the end of 10 minutes, open the lid, fluff the rice with a fork, and garnish with cilantro.

BELL PEPPER RICE

With a handful of spices and a versatile vegetable like the capsicum, this recipe packs in a lot of flavors. It is one you can enjoy all year long.

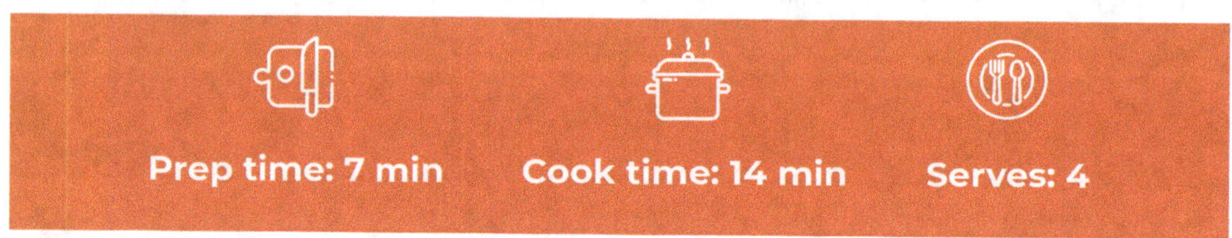

INGREDIENTS

2 cups basmati rice

1 ½ cups water

3 medium bell peppers or capsicum, chopped

1 onion, chopped

¼ cup frozen or fresh corn

2 teaspoons bisi bele bath powder

½ teaspoon garam masala

2 tablespoons mint leaves, chopped

½ teaspoon red chili powder

DRY SPICES

1 mace

2 star anise

2 cardamoms

¼ inch cinnamon stick

2 cloves (spice)

½ teaspoon mustard seed

½ teaspoon cumin seed

½ teaspoon Bengal gram dal

INSTRUCTIONS

1. Press 'sauté' and add a couple of teaspoons of oil to inner pot.

2. When the oil heats up, add cumin seeds, mustard, and Bengal gram dal. Sauté until the dal turns a golden color.

3. Add the other spices listed such as cinnamon, mace, cloves, cardamoms, and a couple of star anise. Sauté for 20 seconds.

4. Add ginger/garlic paste and sliced onions and sauté them for 1 minute.

5. Add chopped capsicum (bell pepper) and frozen corn. Stir well.

6. Add remaining spice powders and continue to stir well to ensure none of the ingredients stick to the pan.

7. Add the rinsed rice, salt, and water and continue to stir for about 1 minute.

8. Top with chopped mint leaves and close lid. Press 'cancel.'

9. Close lid and turn valve from 'venting' to 'sealing' position.
10. Set pot to 'manual/pressure cook' on high pressure and set the timer to 4 minutes.
11. At the end of 4 minutes, let pressure drop gradually by using the 'natural pressure release' (NPR) option. Wait for silver button on lid to drop before opening.
12. Capsicum rice is ready to be served with a side of raita (side dish made of yogurt with raw or cooked vegetables) or Indian mango pickle.

JEERA RICE

Jeera rice or cumin rice is one of the oldest recipes for flavored Indian rice. It is just fluffy rice steam cooked with cumin and other spices. As simple as it sounds, the dish is complete only when you find the right complement to pair it with.

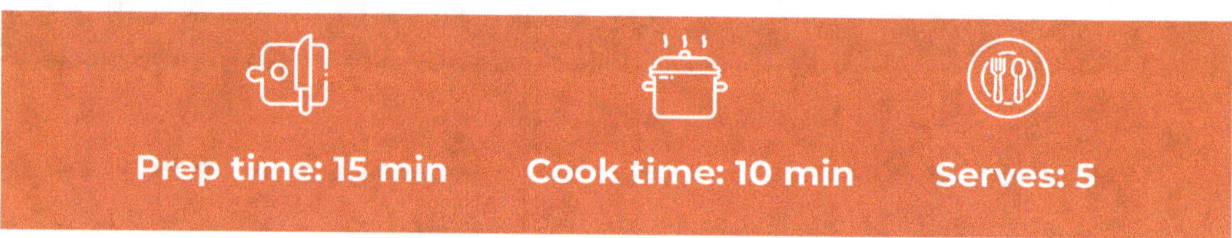

INGREDIENTS

2 cups long grain basmati rice

2 tablespoons vegan butter or coconut oil

3 teaspoons cumin seeds

4 green cardamoms, crushed

4 cloves (spice)

2 bay leaves

3 green chilies, chopped

½ inch cinnamon stick

salt to taste

INSTRUCTIONS

1. Wash basmati rice with clean water to remove all the starch, and then soak in water for 15 to 30 minutes.
2. Add vegan butter or oil to inner pot, and press 'sauté.'
3. As the oil heats up, add cumin seeds, cloves, cardamom, and bay leaf. Sauté for 30 seconds.
4. Add green chilies and cinnamon stick, and continue to stir for at least another 10 to 15 seconds.
5. Add the soaked and drained basmati rice along with salt. Mix well.
6. Add 2 ¼ cups water and give it a good stir one last time.
7. Close lid and turn 'steam release' handle to 'sealing' position.
8. Select 'high pressure' cooking option, and set timer for 4 minutes.
9. When time is up, open lid using natural release.
10. Jeera rice is ready! Serve hot with a side of dal or Indian curries.

SPINACH RICE

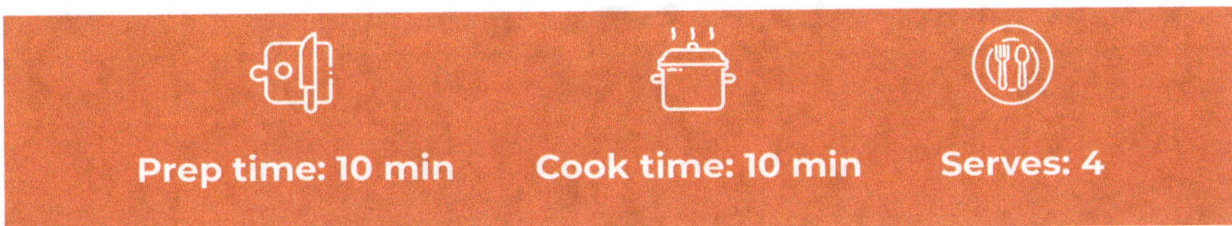

INGREDIENTS

1 ¼ cups basmati rice
2 ½ cups spinach, chopped
⅓ cup frozen peas
2 teaspoons cooking oil
1 teaspoon lemon juice
1 onion, chopped
1 teaspoon ginger, grated
2 garlic cloves, chopped
1 ½ cups water
salt to taste
½ teaspoon red chili powder
½ teaspoon garam masala
¼ teaspoon cumin powder
½ teaspoon coriander powder
¼ inch cinnamon stick

INSTRUCTIONS

1. Press 'sauté' and add 2 teaspoons of oil to inner pot on medium setting.
2. Once it's hot, add cinnamon sticks, chopped ginger/garlic and sauté for 2 minutes until they turn light brown.
3. Add chopped onions and continue to sauté until they turn translucent.
4. Add the spices one by one—red chili powder, garam masala, cumin powder, and coriander powder.
5. Add spinach leaves and frozen green peas and continue to stir well.
6. Add the rinsed basmati rice, water, and salt and give a good stir.
7. Press 'cancel' to stop sautéing. Close lid.
8. Press 'pressure cook' and set timer for 4 minutes on 'high pressure.'
9. After the time expires, do a natural pressure release, remove the lid, add lemon juice, and lightly fluff rice with a fork.
10. Spinach rice is ready! Serve hot and pair with raita.

VEGETABLE BIRYANI

INGREDIENTS

2 cups basmati rice
1 tablespoon vegan butter or oil

WHOLE SPICES

2 green cardamoms
4 cloves (spice)
2 maces
1 bay leaf
3 star anise
½ inch cinnamon stick
½ teaspoon cumin seeds

GROUND SPICES

1 teaspoon coriander powder
½ teaspoon cumin powder
½ - 1 teaspoon red chili powder
1 teaspoon garam masala
¼ teaspoon turmeric powder

OTHER INGREDIENTS

1 cup potatoes, cubed
½ cup carrots, chopped
½ cup beans, chopped
½ cup of frozen corn or peas
1 onion, sliced lengthwise
1 teaspoon ginger, grated
2 garlic cloves, minced
1 ¾ cups water
½ cup vegan yogurt or regular yogurt
1 tablespoon nutritional yeast (optional)
cilantro leaves, chopped
mint leaves, chopped

INSTRUCTIONS

1. Soak basmati rice for 10 to 15 minutes after a good rinse.
2. Press 'sauté' and add vegan butter or oil to inner pan.
3. As oil heats up, add cumin seeds, cinnamon, cardamom, mace, cloves, bay leaf, and star anise.
4. As the cumin seeds fry, add sliced onions and ginger/garlic paste. Sauté for 2 to 3 minutes with regular stirring until they turn light brown in color.

5. Add salt and mixed vegetables of your choice and cook for 20 to 30 seconds.
6. Add coconut yogurt, chopped cilantro, mint leaves, and the spice mix (turmeric powder, red chili powder, cumin, and garam masala powder). Stir well and continue to cook for 30 seconds.
7. Add nutritional yeast, rinsed basmati rice, and water. Give a good stir for an even mix.
8. Press 'cancel.'
9. Close lid and turn valve from 'venting' to 'sealing' position.
10. Set pot to 'manual/pressure cook' on high pressure and set the timer to 5 minutes, cooking with 'natural pressure release' (NPR) option. (Wait for silver button on lid to drop before opening.)
11. Vegetable biryani is ready! Serve it hot, paired with raita and cucumber.

PAGE 58 VEGETABLE BIRYANI

VEGETABLE PULAO

Prep time: 10 mins

Cook time: 20 mins

Serves: 4

INGREDIENTS

2 teaspoons olive oil
2 cloves (spice)
2 star anise
2 green cardamoms
1 bay leaf
1 teaspoon crushed black pepper
1 teaspoon ginger, grated
2 garlic cloves, chopped
1 onion, chopped
salt to taste
1 cup mixed vegetables, chopped
2 cups basmati rice
¼ cup coconut milk
2 ¼ cups water

INSTRUCTIONS

1. Soak basmati rice for 10 minutes.
2. Press 'sauté' and add 2 teaspoons of oil to inner pot set on medium heat.
3. Add whole spices one by one and sauté for 30 seconds.
4. Add grated ginger, chopped onion, and garlic. Sauté until onions turn translucent.
5. Add your choice of chopped vegetables like carrots, beans, and peas. Sauté for 1 minute. Add salt.
6. Add coconut milk, soaked and rinsed basmati rice (add after drained), and add water. Give a nice stir.
7. Press 'cancel' to stop sautéing and close lid.
8. Press 'pressure cook' and set timer for 5 minutes on high pressure.
9. After the time expires, do a natural pressure release, remove the lid, add lemon juice, and lightly fluff rice with a fork.
10. Enjoy vegetable pulao with raita or korma.

BEETROOT RICE

This beet rice is a very simple dish that qualifies for any day. I make this for potluck parties, lunch boxes, and for picnics too.

INGREDIENTS

2 - 3 teaspoons coconut oil

½ teaspoon cumin seeds

2 green cardamoms

1 teaspoon ginger, grated

2 garlic cloves, chopped

1 cup onion, chopped

½ teaspoon chili powder (medium spice level)

½ teaspoon garam masala powder

2 cups beets, grated

2 cups basmati rice

2 ½ cups water

salt to taste (I use 2 teaspoons pink salt)

INSTRUCTIONS

1. Soak basmati rice for 10 minutes.
2. Press 'sauté' and set to normal heat.
3. Add 2 teaspoons of oil to inner pot on medium setting.
4. Add cumin seeds and cardamom. Sauté until cumin starts to sizzle.
5. Add chopped garlic, onion, and grated ginger. Sauté until onion turns translucent.
6. Add red chili powder, garam masala, and salt. Sauté for 30 seconds.
7. Add grated beets. Mix well. Add soaked and drained basmati rice and 2 ½ cups of water. Give a nice stir.
8. Press 'cancel' to stop sautéing and close lid.
9. Press 'pressure cook' and set timer for 4 minutes on high pressure.
10. After the timer expires, do a natural pressure release.
11. Remove lid, add chopped cilantro (if you desire), and lightly fluff rice with a fork.
12. Enjoy the beet rice with vegan raita.

CARROT RICE

Carrot rice or pulao is yet another flavorful rice dish. This is simple yet packed with flavor. Perfect for kids' lunch boxes and picnics.

INGREDIENTS

2 teaspoons olive oil
¼ teaspoon cumin seeds
1 green cardamom, crushed
2 star anise
½ inch cinnamon stick
salt to taste
1 teaspoon ginger, grated
1 garlic clove, grated
1 small onion or 1 cup onion, chopped
1 cup carrots, grated
¼ cup frozen peas (optional)
1 cup basmati rice
1 ¼ cups water

INSTRUCTIONS

1. Wash and rinse basmati rice. Soak until it is added to the pot.
2. Press 'sauté' and add oil. When oil heats up, add cumin seeds, green cardamom, star anise, and cinnamon sticks. Sauté for 20 seconds or until you get the spice aroma.
3. Add chopped onions, ginger, and garlic. Sauté until softened.
4. Add grated carrots and frozen peas. Mix well.
5. Add salt and drained basmati rice and water. Give it a nice stir.
6. Press 'cancel' so you can stop sauté mode.
7. Close lid, press the pressure cook button, and keep it 4 minutes on high pressure.
8. Once the timer is done, keep it closed until pressure is naturally released.
9. Open the lid once the pressure cooking value pin is dropped down.
10. Garnish rice with cilantro if you desire. Serve carrot rice with raita or kurma.

COCONUT RICE

When you are in a hurry and want to serve flavorful rice or pack a lunch box, make this coconut rice and serve with sambar or kurma.

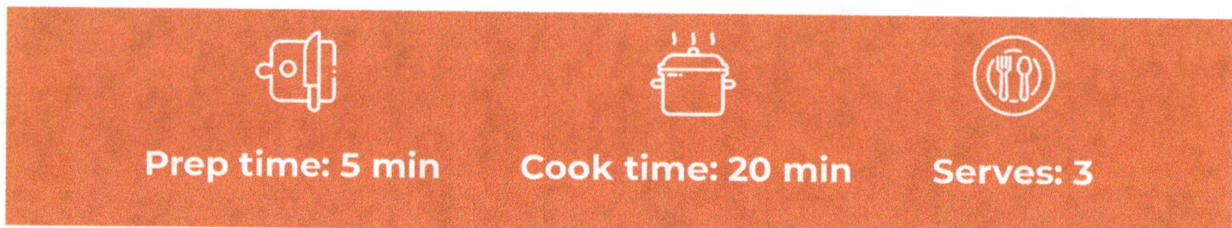

INGREDIENTS

2 teaspoons oil
1 teaspoon mustard seeds
½ teaspoon cumin seeds
1 teaspoon ginger, grated
1 green chili, chopped
1 strand curry leaf
salt to taste
⅓ cup frozen peas (optional)
1 cup sona masoori rice
1 ½ cups canned coconut milk
1 cup water

INSTRUCTIONS

1. Wash and rinse rice well. Keep it aside.
2. Press the 'sauté' buttonand add oil. When oil is hot, add mustard seeds and cumin seeds. Sauté for 20 seconds.
3. Add grated ginger and green chilies. Sauté for another 20 seconds.
4. Add frozen peas, salt, and rinsed and drained rice. Mix well.
5. Add coconut milk and water. Give it a nice stir.
6. Press 'cancel.' Place lid and close the 'pressure-release' valve. Adjust to 'pressure cook' on high for 7 minutes.
7. Let the pressure release for 10 minutes naturally, then do a quick release. Open the lid after pressure is released.
8. Garnish with cilantro. Fluff the rice with a fork. Coconut rice is ready to enjoy.

Quinoa and millet are great rice alternatives for anyone looking to reduce calorie intake. The possibilities are endless with these wonder grains, so whether you're looking to add some new healthy items to your pantry or trying to find an alternative grain, these two make great choices!

MUSHROOM QUINOA

Prep Time: 8 min   **Cook Time: 6 min**   **Serves: 4**

INGREDIENTS

12 ounces mushrooms, sliced
1 ½ cups quinoa
1 ½ cups water or vegetable broth
1 onion, chopped
¼ cup frozen peas
2 garlic cloves, chopped
½ teaspoon red chili powder or cayenne powder
¼ teaspoon turmeric powder
¼ teaspoon cinnamon powder
¼ teaspoon garam masala
¼ teaspoon black pepper
cilantro for garnishing (optional)

INSTRUCTIONS

1. Wash the quinoa in cold water. Rinse, drain, and set it aside.
2. Press 'sauté' and add oil to inner pot.
3. As oil heats up, add chopped garlic. Sauté for 1 minute.
4. Add sliced, cleaned mushrooms. Sauté for another minute.
5. Add sliced onions. Sauté until they turn translucent.
6. Add frozen peas, all the spices, and salt. Mix well. Sauté for 30 seconds to 1 minute.
7. Add prewashed quinoa or rinsed quinoa followed up with 1 ½ cups water. Stir well, then press 'cancel.'
8. Close lid, press 'pressure cooker,' set the valve to 'sealing' mode, and set the timer for 3 minutes.
9. At the end of the timer, let the pressure release naturally before opening the lid.
10. Fluff the quinoa lightly with a fork and garnish with cilantro if desired. Mushroom quinoa is ready to enjoy.

QUINOA UPMA

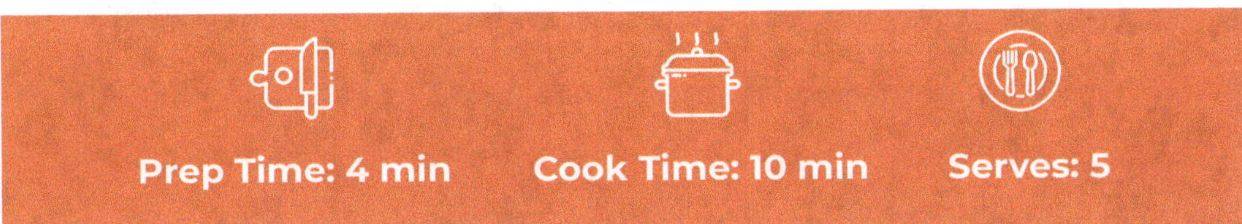

INGREDIENTS

2 cups quinoa

2 ½ cups water

2 carrots, chopped

¼ cup frozen peas

1 tomato, chopped

1 strand curry leaves

1 teaspoon ginger, grated

2 green chilies, sliced

2 tablespoons oil

3 tablespoons cashew nuts

½ teaspoon mustard seeds

½ teaspoon urad dal or split
   black gram

1 red chili, halved

1 teaspoon lemon juice

cilantro leaves for garnishing
   (optional)

INSTRUCTIONS

1. Wash the quinoa in cold water. Rinse, drain, and set it aside.
2. Press 'sauté' and add cooking oil to inner pot.
3. When oil heats up, add mustard seeds, urad dal, and red chili. Sauté until mustard seeds sizzle.
4. Add curry leaves, cashews, ginger, and green chilies. Sauté for up to 30 seconds.
5. Add chopped tomatoes and stir occasionally to make sure it doesn't stick to the inner pot. Add the chopped carrots and frozen peas. Mix well.
6. Add rinsed quinoa, salt, and water to inner pot.
7. Close lid and press 'cancel.'
8. Press the 'pressure cook' option and cook for 2 minutes.
9. Once the timer is done, wait until the pressure is naturally released.
10. Open lid and fluff quinoa with a fork. Add lemon juice, garnish with cilantro (optional). Quinoa upma is ready! Serve hot with chai.

VEGETABLE QUINOA

Prep Time: 10 min   **Cook Time: 4 min**   **Serves: 4**

INGREDIENTS

1 ½ cups white quinoa

2 tablespoons cooking oil

1 teaspoon cumin seeds

4 cloves (spice)

2 star anise (optional)

1 bay leaf (optional)

1 teaspoon garlic cloves, minced

2 teaspoons ginger paste or
   ginger, chopped

1 small onion, chopped

1 tomato, chopped

1 potato, cubed

1 cup green beans, chopped

1 carrot, chopped

¼ teaspoon turmeric powder

½ teaspoon black pepper
   powder (optional)

½ teaspoon red chili powder

1 teaspoon garam masala

pink salt to taste

¼ cup coconut milk

1 ½ cups water

2 tablespoons chopped cilantro
   (optional)

INSTRUCTIONS

1. Wash the quinoa in cold water. Rinse, drain and set it aside.
2. Press 'sauté' and add oil to inner pot. When oil is hot, add cumin seeds, star anise, and cloves.
3. Add the following in the same order with a minute of cooking time between each: minced ginger, garlic, onions, tomatoes, and all dry spices.
4. Add all the vegetables, coconut milk, and salt. Stir constantly for 30 seconds.
5. Add rinsed quinoa and water and continue to stir.
6. Close lid. Turn 'steam release' handle to 'sealing' position. Press 'pressure cook' and set the time for 4 minutes.
7. When time is up, open lid after 10 minutes of natural pressure release.
8. Vegetable quinoa is ready to serve!

LEMON QUINOA

INGREDIENTS

1 cup quinoa
1 ½ cups water
3 tablespoons peanuts, whole
1 teaspoon cumin seeds
2 teaspoons ginger, grated
2 green chilies, chopped
2 teaspoons coconut oil
cilantro for garnish (optional)
2 tablespoons lemon juice

INSTRUCTIONS

1. Wash the quinoa in cold water. Rinse, drain, and set it aside.
2. Press 'sauté' and add a few teaspoons of oil to inner pot.
3. As oil heats up, add peanuts. Sauté until they start to turn crispy.
4. Add cumin seeds and sauté until they start to sizzle.
5. Add grated ginger and chopped green chilies and cook for about 30 seconds.
6. Add the rinsed quinoa, salt to taste, and turmeric powder.
7. Add water in the right proportion as noted in the ingredients list. Stir well.
8. Close the lid, and turn the steam release handle to 'sealing' position. Press 'manual/pressure cook' and set timer for 2 minutes.
9. As time expires, use the natural release to let the pressure settle, and then open the lid.
10. Add lemon juice and cilantro (optional). Mix well. Lemon quinoa is ready to serve.

QUINOA KHICHDI

If you like the khichdi recipe, then I assure you this quinoa khichdi will be your next favorite. Made with simple spices and vegetables.

INGREDIENTS

2 teaspoons coconut oil

½ teaspoon cumin seeds

2 garlic cloves, chopped

1 teaspoon ginger, grated

½ cup onions, chopped

1 tomato, chopped

¼ cup carrots, chopped

¼ cup frozen or fresh peas

¼ teaspoon turmeric powder

½ teaspoon mild spicy red chili powder

½ teaspoon garam masala powder

½ cup quinoa

¼ cup masoor dal/red lentil

¼ cup split yellow lentil/moong dal

2 ½ cups water (for thinner consistency, add 3 cups of water)

INSTRUCTIONS

1. Wash quinoa and lentils in running water. Rinse well and set aside.
2. Set to 'sauté' and add a few teaspoons of oil to inner pot.
3. Add cumin seeds when it starts to sizzle. Add chopped garlic and grated ginger. Sauté for 20 seconds.
4. Add chopped onions. Sauté until onions turn soft.
5. Add chopped tomatoes, salt, and other vegetables like carrots and peas. Cook for 1 minute.
6. Add all the spice powders one by one. Mix well.
7. Add rinsed and drained quinoa and lentils. Add water and give it a nice stir. Press the 'cancel' button.
8. Close lid and turn steam release handle to 'sealing' position. Press 'manual/pressure cook' and set timer for 5 minutes.
9. As time expires, use natural release to let the pressure settle, and then open lid.
10. Garnish with cilantro if desired. Serve warm. Enjoy with plain yogurt or Indian pickle.

MILLET UPMA

 **Prep Time: 5 min**  **Cook Time: 12 min**  **Soak Time: 2 hr**  **Serves: 3**

INGREDIENTS

1 cup proso millet

1 ¾ cups water

1 small onion, chopped

1 tomato, chopped

½ cup frozen vegetables of your choice

1 teaspoon mustard seeds

1 teaspoon urad dal

1 red chili, halved

½ teaspoon red chili powder

⅓ teaspoon garam masala

¼ teaspoon turmeric

salt to taste

1 strand curry leaves

2 teaspoons ginger, grated

2 teaspoons coconut oil

2 teaspoons lemon juice

cilantro for garnish (optional)

INSTRUCTIONS

1. Soak rinsed millet for 2 hours, and then drain completely and place aside.
2. On 'sauté' setting, add a few teaspoons of oil to inner pot.
3. As oil heats up, add mustard seeds, urad dal, and red chili. Sauté until they start to sizzle.
4. Add grated ginger and curry leaves. Cook for about 30 seconds.
5. Add chopped onions. Sauté until they are translucent.
6. Add chopped tomatoes. Mix well, then add the dry spices: red chili powder, turmeric, and garam masala. Continue to stir well to cook the tomatoes completely.
7. Add frozen vegetables of your choice. I use green peas and green beans.
8. Add salt and mix thoroughly.
9. Add soaked and drained millet. Add water in the right proportion as noted in the ingredients list. Stir well.
10. Close lid and turn the steam release handle to 'sealing' position. Press 'manual/pressure cook' and set timer for 8-10 minutes.
11. As time expires, use the natural release to let the pressure settle, and then open the lid.
12. Add lemon juice and cilantro. Mix well. Millet upma is ready to serve.

MILLET PULAO

Millet pulao is typically made with Indian spices, vegetables, and proso millet, but you can also use barnyard millet, little millet, and Kodo millet.

Prep Time: 5 min

Cook Time: 25 min

Soak Time: 45 min   Serves: 4

INGREDIENTS

1 teaspoon olive oil

½ teaspoon cumin seeds

3 cloves (spice)

2 star anise

1 bay leaf

1 cardamom

1 onion, chopped

1 teaspoon ginger, grated

2 garlic cloves, minced

¼ teaspoon turmeric powder

¼ teaspoon red chili powder (mildly spicy)

½ teaspoon garam masala

2 teaspoons mint leaves, chopped

1.2 cups beans, chopped

¼ cup frozen peas

1 carrot, chopped

1 cup proso millet

1 ¾ cups water

2 teaspoons cilantro, chopped (optional for garnish)

INSTRUCTIONS

1. Wash millet 4 times or until water runs clear. Soak for 45 minutes in plenty of water. Once done, rinse again, and drain all the water.

2. Press 'sauté' and heat oil. Once the oil gets hot, add the bay leaves, cloves, cardamom, and star anise. Sauté for 30 seconds.

3. Add sliced onion and sauté for about 2 minutes or until the onions turn soft and light brown.

4. Add chopped ginger and garlic and sauté for 1 minute.

5. Add the powdered spices: red chili powder, turmeric powder (optional), and garam masala. Sauté for 15 seconds.

6. Add the veggies and salt, and coat them with all the masala.

7. Add the drained millet, and gently mix with the other ingredients for about 30 seconds.

8. Add the water and mint leaves. Give a mix, making sure you deglaze the pot. Taste the broth and adjust the salt.

9. Close the lid and adjust the vent to 'sealing.' 'Pressure cook' on high for 8 minutes. After the Instant Pot beeps, wait 5 minutes before you release the rest of the pressure. Gently fluff the pulao and let it rest for 5 minutes.

10. Add lemon juice and garnish with cilantro. Serve the millet pulao with plain yogurt or raita.

MILLET PONGAL

Millet Pongal is a nutritious, simple, comfort food, perfect for breakfast and lunch. Serve with coconut chutney or sambar.

INGREDIENTS

1 cup millet (use any small variety like proso millet, little millet, or foxtail millet)

¾ cup moong dal

5 cups water

1 teaspoon cumin seeds

2 teaspoons black pepper

3 tablespoons cashews, chopped

2 tablespoons coconut oil or olive oil

¼ teaspoon turmeric powder

2 teaspoons ginger, grated

1 strand curry leaves

1 ½ teaspoons pink salt

INSTRUCTIONS

1. Rinse millet in clean water 3 times, then soak in water for 2 to 3 hours.
2. Wash and rinse the moong dal or yellow split lentils 3 times. Set aside.
3. Press 'sauté' and add oil to inner pot. When oil is hot, add cumin seeds, black pepper, and cashews. Sauté until the cashews are golden.
4. Add grated ginger, curry leaves, and turmeric powder. Sauté for 10 seconds.
5. Add drained millet and moong dal. Mix well.
6. Add salt and water. Give it a nice stir. Press 'cancel' to stop 'sauté' mode.
7. Close lid and adjust vent to 'sealing' position.
8. Press 'pressure cook' and cook for 8 minutes.
9. When the cooking time is done, press 'cancel' and let the pressure release naturally. Open lid after pin is dropped down.
10. Enjoy millet Pongal with coconut chutney.

Sambar and dal can replace a meal with their nutritional contribution. Although they hail from different parts of India, sambar and dal recipes find a common ground in the fact that they are both rich in lentils and hence are high in protein. Sambar pairs well with rice, while dal pairs well with whole wheat flatbread (chapati). They are all truly comfort foods, in the same vein as split pea soup. Enjoy over hot cooked rice with a simple vegetable side for a filling vegan meal.

INSTANT POT SAMBAR

Prep time: 7 min

Cook time: 20 min

Serves: 5

INGREDIENTS

1 tablespoon cooking oil

½ teaspoon mustard seeds

1 red chili, halved

½ teaspoon urad dal

2 green chilies, sliced

7 curry leaves

1 red or white onion, chopped

2 tomatoes, chopped

¼ teaspoon turmeric powder

2 tablespoons sambar powder

2 red potatoes, cubed

1 carrot, chopped

¾ cup pigeon pea/toor dal

2 ½ cups water

salt to taste

½ teaspoon tamarind
   concentrate or 2 teaspoons
   lemon juice

1 teaspoon jaggery or brown
   sugar

INSTRUCTIONS

1. Press 'sauté' and add oil to inner pot. When oil is hot, add mustard seeds and urad dal.

2. As the mustard seeds start to sputter, add curry leaves and green chilies. Stir well for 1 minute.

3. Add onions and continue to sauté for at least 1 more minute.

4. Add tomatoes, let them soften up, then add potatoes. In about a minute, add turmeric and sambar powder and stir well for an even mixture.

5. Add toor dal, tamarind or lemon juice, jaggery, water, and salt.

6. Close lid. Turn steam release handle to 'sealing' position. Press 'pressure cook' on high and set the timer for 6 minutes.

7. When time is up, open lid using the 'quick release' option or you can also let it cool down naturally.

8. Garnish with cilantro if desired. Sambar is ready!

BRINJAL (EGGPLANT) SAMBAR

 **Prep time: 10 min**  **Cook time: 10 min**  **Serves: 4**

INGREDIENTS

6 to 8 small purple brinjals (eggplant)

½ cup toor dal

1 medium-sized onion, chopped

4 green chilies, sliced

2 tablespoons sambar powder

½ teaspoon turmeric powder

small lemon-sized tamarind or 1 tablespoon tamarind paste

5 small curry leaves

2 red chilies, halved (optional)

1 teaspoon mustard seeds

1 teaspoon split black gram

1 tablespoon oil

2 teaspoons grated jaggery (or use brown powder)

INSTRUCTIONS

1. Press 'sauté' and add oil to inner pot.
2. As oil heats up, add mustard seeds and urad dal.
3. When mustard seeds start to sputter, add curry leaves and green chili. Stir well for 1 minute.
4. Add onions and continue to sauté for at least 1 minute.
5. Add brinjal pieces, turmeric, and sambar powder. Stir well for an even mixture.
6. Add split toor dal (split pigeon pea), tamarind, water, and salt.
7. Close lid. Turn steam release handle to 'sealing' position. Press 'pressure cook' and set timer for 6 minutes.
8. When time is up, open lid using the 10 minutes natural release option.
9. Garnish with cilantro. Brinjal (eggplant) sambar is ready! Pair with steamed rice, dosa, or idli.

RADISH SAMBAR

Radish sambar is made with toor/pigeon pea lentils and roasted whole spices. Serve with plain cooked basmati rice.

INGREDIENTS

1 large white radish or approximately 4 cups, chopped
1 teaspoon coconut oil
1 tomato, chopped
2 green chilies, sliced
¼ teaspoon turmeric powder
2 tablespoons sambar powder
¾ cup toor dal/split pigeon pea
1 teaspoon jaggery powder
1 teaspoon tamarind paste or lemon juice
salt to taste
3 ½ cups water
½ inch cinnamon stick
1 green cardamom
2 cloves (spice)
6 black peppers

TEMPERING INGREDIENTS

1 teaspoon coconut oil
1 teaspoon mustard seeds
½ teaspoon urad dal
1 red chili, halved
pinch of asafoetida
1 strand curry leaves

INSTRUCTIONS

1. Dry roast whole spices (cinnamon, cloves, cardamom, and black pepper) until you get the nice aroma, then powder it using a coffee blender or crush it in the pestle.
2. Press 'sauté' and keep it on 'normal' mode. Add oil. When oil heats up, add chopped radish and tomatoes. Sauté for 1 minute.
3. Add turmeric powder, sambar powder, roasted and powdered spices, and salt, then mix well.

4. Add soaked and drained toor dal/pigeon pea lentil, jaggery, tamarind paste, and water. Give a nice stir.

5. Close lid, press 'cancel,' then press pressure cook button for 6 to 7 minutes on high. Make sure you turn the value into 'sealing' position.

6. Once the cooking time is done, press 'cancel' and let the pressure release naturally.

7. Open lid after the pin drops. Add cilantro and tempering. For tempering: Place a pan over the heat and add oil. When oil heats up, add mustard seeds and urad dal. When mustard seeds start to pop up, add red chili, asafoetida, and curry leaves.

8. Mix well. Turn off heat. Add tempering to sambar.

SPINACH DAL

Prep time: 5 min   Cook time: 20 min   Soak time: 30 min   Serves: 4

INGREDIENTS

12 to 14 ounces fresh spinach, chopped

⅓ cup toor dal

¼ cup chana dal

¼ cup moong dal

1 ¾ cups water to 2 cups water (stovetop pressure cooker)

1 onion, chopped

2 garlic cloves, chopped

½ inch ginger, grated

1 green chili, sliced (optional)

1 tablespoon coconut oil

1 teaspoon cumin seeds

3 cloves (spice), crushed

salt to taste

1 teaspoon coriander powder

½ teaspoon red chili powder

¼ teaspoon turmeric powder

½ teaspoon garam masala

2 teaspoons lemon juice

¼ teaspoon kasuri methi

2 teaspoons oil for tempering

INSTRUCTIONS

1. Add lentils and add water until it covers completely. Cook for 15 minutes on high pressure.

2. Place a pan over medium heat and drizzle 1 tablespoon coconut oil. When oil heats up, add cumin seeds and cloves. When they start to sizzle, add chopped garlic and ginger, and after 10 to 15 seconds, add green chilies (optional). Stir for a few seconds.

3. Add chopped onions and continue to cook until onions turn transparent.

4. Add turmeric powder, garam masala, coriander powder (dhania powder), chili powder, and salt. Continue to stir well. Cover lid for about 1 minute.

5. Add chopped spinach or add baby spinach without chopping, add ¼ cup water, stir well, and cover lid.

6. After about 3 minutes, add the cooked lentils and add water if it is too dry. When it starts to boil, add lemon juice, simmer down the heat, and cook for about 1 minute. As the spinach cooks thoroughly, switch off the heat.

TEMPERING

1. This step is optional, but I never skip it, as it gives extra flavor and aroma to the spinach dal. Place a small pan over medium heat, and add cooking oil. As the oil heats up, add hing/asafoetida, Kashmiri red chili powder, kasuri methi, 2 dried red chilies, and sauté for 15 seconds. Pour this tadka or tempering to the dal palak and let the flavors spread to the entire dal.
2. Spinach dal is ready! Serve hot and paired with rice or roti for the best tasting nutritious dinner!

DAL FRY

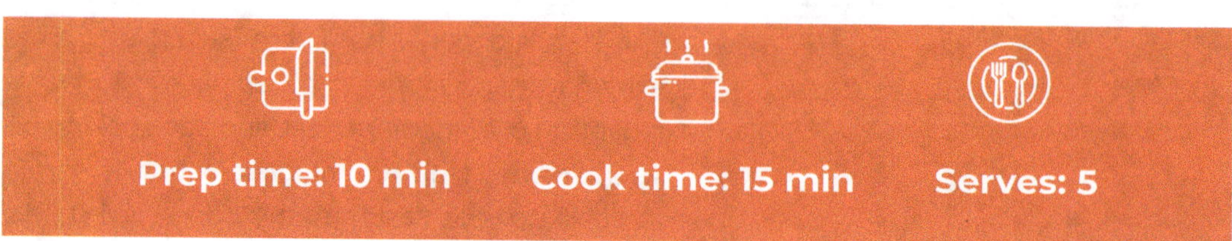

INGREDIENTS

½ teaspoon mustard seeds

½ teaspoon cumin seeds

1 red chili, halved

2 teaspoons ginger garlic paste

1 onion, chopped

1 tomato, chopped or use 1
  tablespoon tomato paste

1 ½ cups pigeon pea lentil or
  Toor dal

½ teaspoon garam masala

¼ teaspoon turmeric powder

½ teaspoon red chili powder

½ teaspoon coriander powder

salt to taste

2 green chilies

1 strand curry leaves (optional)

4 cups water

½ teaspoon fenugreek leaves or
  kasuri methi

cilantro leaves for garnish
  (optional)

INSTRUCTIONS

1. Press 'sauté' and drizzle a couple of teaspoons of oil.

2. As the oil heats up, add mustard seeds and cumin seeds and after a few seconds, add chopped or minced garlic and ginger.

3. Once the cumin seeds start to sizzle and the garlic changes color, add onions, ginger, and green chilies. Sauté for 2 minutes.

4. Add tomatoes, spices (turmeric, coriander powder, chili powder) and stir them well. Follow it up with Toor dal (pigeon pea lentil) and water for cooking. Stir it all up.

5. Press 'cancel' and close lid with valve in 'sealing' position.

6. Change setting to 'manual/pressure cook' mode at high pressure for 6 minutes.

7. When the Instant Pot beeps, let the pressure release naturally.

8. Add garam masala and fenugreek leaves. Give a good stir. Garnish with cilantro, then serve with rice or roti.

CHANA DAL

 **Prep time: 30 min** 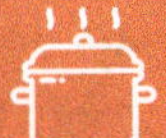 **Cook time: 20 min**  **Serves: 5**

INGREDIENTS

2 cups chana dal/split Bengal gram

4 to 4 ½ cups water

2 medium-sized tomatoes, chopped

1 onion, chopped

2 teaspoons ginger, grated

2 garlic cloves, minced

2 green chilies, chopped

1 teaspoon cumin seeds

1 red chili, halved

½ teaspoon cumin powder

1 teaspoon coriander powder

½ teaspoon to 1 teaspoon red chili powder or cayenne powder

1 teaspoon mango powder/ amchur

2 teaspoons dry fenugreek/ dry methi leaves

4 to 6 teaspoons coconut oil

salt to taste

cilantro for garnish (optional)

INSTRUCTIONS

1. Soak chana dal for 30 minutes in water, then drain and set aside.
2. Press 'sauté' mode and drizzle a couple of teaspoons of oil.
3. As the oil heats up, add the cumin seeds. After a few seconds, add chopped or minced garlic.
4. Once the cumin seeds start to sizzle and the garlic changes color, add onions, ginger, and green chilies. Sauté for 2 minutes.
5. Add tomatoes and spices. Stir well. Follow up with chana dal and water for cooking. Stir it all up.
6. Press 'cancel' and close lid with a vent in 'sealing' position.
7. Change setting to 'manual/pressure cook' mode at high pressure for 10 to 12 minutes.
8. When the Instant Pot beeps, let the pressure release naturally.
9. Add tempering and give a good stir. (For tempering, heat oil in a small pan, and sauté 1 red chili, chili powder, fenugreek leaves/ kasoori methi and add into the dal)
10. Garnish with cilantro, then serve with rice or roti.

RED LENTIL DAL

Red lentil dal is made with masoor dal and cooked deeply with spices. Serve with a bowl of rice and stir fry vegetables.

Prep time: 10 min

Cook time: 20 min

Serves: 6

INGREDIENTS

1 tablespoon coconut oil

1 teaspoon cumin seeds

1 onion, chopped

2 garlic cloves, chopped

2 teaspoons ginger, grated

2 cloves, crushed

2 green chilies, chopped

2 tablespoons tomato paste

¼ teaspoon turmeric powder

1 teaspoon coriander powder

1 teaspoon garam masala

1 teaspoon Kashmiri red chili powder

2 teaspoons pink salt

2 cups masoor dal/red lentil

6 cups water

2 teaspoons crushed kasuri methi (optional)

INSTRUCTIONS

1. Press 'sauté' mode and drizzle 2 teaspoons of oil in inner pot.
2. As oil heats up, add the cumin seeds and crushed cloves. Sauté for 20 seconds.
3. Add chopped onions, chopped chilies, grated ginger, and chopped garlic. Sauté until onions turn translucent.
4. Add tomato paste and water. Deglaze the pot and keep stirring because the paste will get stuck in the inner pot.
5. Add turmeric powder, coriander, and garam masala powder and keep stirring.
6. Add rinsed masoor dal and salt, and add remaining water. Give a nice stir.
7. Press 'cancel' and close the lid with the vent in 'sealing' position.
8. Change setting to 'manual pressure cook' mode at high pressure for 6 minutes.
9. When the Instant Pot beeps, let the pressure release naturally.
10. Open the lid, add kasuri methi and chopped cilantro, and mix well. Enjoy the warm red lentil along with rice or roti.

GREEN MOONG DAL

Green moong dal has been around for years, yet its popularity is not close to what it deserves. With a full serving of rich, high-quality protein in every bite, green moong dal is one of the most inexpensive super-foods on the market today.

INGREDIENTS

1 cup dry whole green moong dal/green gram

1 onion, chopped

2 small tomatoes, chopped

2 green chilies, chopped

2 teaspoons ginger, grated

salt to taste

1 tablespoon coconut oil

1 teaspoon cumin seeds/jeera

½ teaspoon mustard seeds

1 teaspoon grated turmeric root (or use ¼ teaspoon turmeric powder)

1 teaspoon coriander powder

½ teaspoon cumin powder

1 - 2 teaspoons red chili powder (adjust to your spice level)

3 teaspoons lemon juice

2 tablespoons coriander leaves/cilantro (optional)

INSTRUCTIONS

1. If you have the time, rinse and soak green mung beans for at least 4 hours. If you don't have time, use unsoaked beans, but make sure to adjust the time (cook 20 to 25 minutes)

2. Press the sauté button, keep it in the medium setting, and add oil. When oil heats up, add mustard seeds and cumin seeds. Sauté until the spices start sizzling.

3. Add grated ginger and chopped chilies. Sauté for 15 to 30 seconds.

4. Add chopped onions. Sauté until they turn translucent.

5. Add chopped tomatoes. Sauté until softened.

6. Add the spices: red chili powder, cumin powder, coriander powder, turmeric powder or grated turmeric root, and salt, and continue to sauté. Mix well.

7. Add soaked and drained whole moong dal and 1 ¾ cups water. Stir well.

8. Press 'cancel' to stop sautéing. Close lid.
9. Press 'pressure cook' and set timer for 6 minutes on high pressure. When Instant Pot beeps, let the pressure release naturally. It is safe to open the lid only after the pin drops down.
10. Open lid, add fresh lemon juice and cilantro. Mix well.
11. Green Moong Dal curry is ready to serve.

PANCHMEL DAL

Panchmel dal is nothing but a dal recipe made with 5 lentils and Indian spices. This is a protein-packed dal recipe.

INGREDIENTS

2 teaspoons oil
½ teaspoon cumin seeds
2 teaspoons ginger, grated
3 garlic cloves, chopped
1 onion, chopped
 2 tomatoes, chopped
¼ teaspoon turmeric powder
1 teaspoon coriander powder
½ teaspoon red chili powder
½ teaspoon garam masala
¼ cup toor dal
¼ cup masoor dal
¼ cup chana dal
¼ cup urad dal
¼ cup moong dal
4 cups water

TEMPERING INGREDIENTS

1 teaspoon oil
2 teaspoons kasuri methi
½ teaspoon Kashmiri red chili powder
¼ teaspoon asafoetida/hing powder

INSTRUCTIONS

1. Wash and rinse all the lentils in clean water until you see clear water, then set aside.
2. Press 'sauté' and add oil. When oil is hot, add cumin seeds and sauté for 10 seconds.
3. Add chopped onions, grated ginger, and garlic. Sauté until onions turn soft.
4. Add chopped tomatoes and salt. Sauté 20 seconds.
5. Add all the dry spice powders one by one. Sauté for 20 seconds.
6. Add the drained lentils and water. Give it a nice stir.
7. Cancel sauté function. Put on lid.
8. Press 'pressure cook' and set to 8 minutes. When done, do a natural release. Open lid.

9. Add chopped cilantro.
10. Place a small pan over the stovetop and prepare tempering by pouring a teaspoon of oil. When oil is hot, add kasuri methi, red chili powder, and hing powder. Sauté for 10 seconds and pour tempering on panchmel dal.
11. Serve with rice or roti.

DAL MAKHANI

Dal Makhani is an Indian curry that is loved around the world. The creamy texture is so easy to attain when cooked in an Instant Pot. Dal means 'lentils' and makhani means 'butter.' For this recipe, I use vegan butter and coconut cream.

INGREDIENTS

1 tablespoon vegan butter or oil
1 teaspoon cumin seeds
1 bay leaf
1 onion, chopped
3 garlic cloves, minced
1 tablespoon ginger, grated
2 tomatoes, chopped
1 teaspoon Kashmiri red chili powder
¼ teaspoon turmeric powder
1 teaspoon coriander powder
½ teaspoon garam masala
salt to taste
1 cup whole black gram/urad dal
¼ cup green moong dal
¼ cup masoor dal
3 cups water
2 tablespoons coconut cream
cilantro for garnishing (optional)
1 teaspoon lemon juice (optional)

INSTRUCTIONS

1. Wash and rinse urad dal/lentil, soak for 4 to 6 hours.
2. Turn to 'sauté.' When hot, add the vegan butter or oil, bay leaves, and cumin seeds.
3. Once the cumin seeds crackle, add ginger, garlic, and chopped onions. Give it a stir.
4. Sauté for a couple of minutes until the onion becomes soft.
5. Add the tomatoes, salt, turmeric, Kashmiri red chili powder, garam masala, and coriander powder. Mix well.
6. Add lentils/dal. Stir well to mix, and then add 3 cups of water.
7. Cancel the sauté function, put on lid.
8. Press 'pressure cook.' Set for 30 minutes or press the chili/bean button (built-in timer)

9. At the end of 30 minutes, do a natural release and open lid.
10. Add chopped cilantro (if desired) and coconut cream.
11. Serve with naan, jeera rice, or roti.

Vegan Curries

In my 12+ years of cooking curries, they are one of the most delicious types of food! Curries pair well with rice, Indian bread, and even pita bread! It is quite challenging to group all the various possibilities of curries in one category, but the recipes that follow are a good collection of popular dishes you will find in restaurants.

VEGETABLE KURMA

Vegetable kurma is one of the best main courses in a restaurant. You can prepare it with a yogurt or coconut base—this recipe uses coconut.

INGREDIENTS

3 tablespoons olive oil
bay leaf
4 cups fresh vegetables (your
   choice), chopped
1 ½ cups water
salt to taste

INGREDIENTS FOR GRAVY

½ inch cinnamon stick
4 cloves (spice)
2 cardamom pods seeds
1 teaspoon fennel seeds
½ teaspoon cumin seeds
4 teaspoons coriander seeds
¼ teaspoon turmeric powder
1 teaspoon red chili powder
   (medium spicy)
1 inch ginger piece, grated
5 - 7 fresh mint leaves
1 cup coconut, grated

15 cashews, whole
2 teaspoons poppy seeds (optional)
3 fresh tomatoes, chopped
¼ cup water

INSTRUCTIONS

1. Soak cashews and poppy seeds in water for 30 minutes.
2. Place gravy ingredients in a blender. Blend into a smooth paste/sauce. Set it aside.
3. Press 'sauté' and add oil to inner pot. When oil is starting to heat up, add bay leaves.
4. Add blended kurma paste, and sauté on low mode. After 30 seconds, add all the chopped vegetables, salt, and 1 ½ cups water. Mix well, and then press 'cancel.'
5. Close lid, press the pressure cook button, and cook for 1 minute on high pressure. Once the cooking time is done, you can also use the quick release option or open lid until all the pressure is released.
6. Garnish with cilantro (if desired) and serve with paratha, roti, or rice.

EGGPLANT CURRY

INGREDIENTS

12 eggplants or brinjal, chopped

1 to 2 potatoes, cubed

½ cup frozen peas

1 onion, chopped

2 tablespoons tomato paste

1 teaspoon coriander powder

½ teaspoon red chili powder

⅓ teaspoon garam masala

½ inch ginger, grated

1 garlic clove, chopped

2 tablespoons cooking oil

1 cup coconut milk

1 ½ cups water

salt to taste

cilantro for garnish (optional)

INSTRUCTIONS

1. Press 'sauté' to medium. Pour a few teaspoons of oil into inner pot.
2. As oil heats up, fry chopped onions, ginger, and garlic.
3. Add tomato paste. Sauté for 1 minute.
4. Add chopped eggplant, potato, and frozen peas. This is also the time to add all the spice powders, salt, and water. Mix well.
5. Turn off sauté mode and put on 'manual' at high for 3 minutes. Set valve to 'sealing' position.
6. At the end of 3 minutes, use the natural release option to let the ingredients cook, or you can use the quick release option, but you will need to set the timer for 5 minutes instead of 3.
7. After the pressure is released, put it on sauté mode again, then boil for 1 minute after adding coconut milk.
8. Garnish with cilantro strands (if desired) and serve hot and steamy!

LENTIL CURRY

 **Prep time: 5 min**

 **Cook time: 25 min**

 **Serves: 4**

INGREDIENTS

1 ½ cups brown or green whole lentils

3 cups water

1 onion, chopped

2 small tomatoes, chopped

2 garlic cloves, chopped

½ inch ginger, grated

4 cloves (spice), optional

1 bay leaf

1 teaspoon cumin seeds

¼ teaspoon turmeric powder

½ teaspoon garam masala

1 teaspoon cayenne powder

1 teaspoon coriander powder

INSTRUCTIONS

1. Press 'sauté' (medium) and add oil. As oil heats up, add cumin seeds and crushed cloves. Sauté for a few seconds.
2. Add chopped garlic, grated ginger, and chopped onions. Sauté until the onions turn translucent.
3. Add chopped tomatoes. Sauté until soft.
4. Add salt, bay leaf, cayenne, garam masala, and coriander powder. Sauté for 2 to 3 minutes.
5. Add washed and rinsed lentils, add water, and stir well.
6. Press 'cancel,' close lid, and press 'pressure cooker.' Set timer for 15 minutes on high pressure.
7. When the Instant Pot beeps, let the pressure release naturally. It is safe to open the lid only after the pin drops down.
8. Add chopped cilantro and a little lemon juice. Mix well.
9. Enjoy lentil curry paired with rice or quinoa.

CHANA MASALA

Prep time: 8 min   Cook time: 40 min   Soak time: 5 hr   Serves: 6

INGREDIENTS

2 cups dry chickpeas

1 can diced tomatoes (14.5 oz.)
   or 2 tomatoes, chopped

1 onion, chopped

2 teaspoons ginger, grated

2 garlic cloves, minced

1 bay leaf

2 teaspoons red chili powder

¼ teaspoon turmeric powder

1 teaspoon cumin seeds
   (optional)

3 cups water

¼ teaspoon amchur powder

¼ teaspoon kasuri methi

1 tablespoon brown sugar
   (optional)

cilantro for garnish (optional)

INSTRUCTIONS

1. Soak chickpeas in 3 to 4 cups of warm water, and let it sit for at least 4 hours. Drain and set aside.
2. Grind spices in a coffee blender or mixer jar. (skip if you buy chana masala powder from a store)
3. Press 'sauté' (medium) and add oil. As oil heats up, add cumin seeds.
4. When cumin seeds start to sizzle, add chopped onions. Sauté until they turn translucent.
5. Add ginger and garlic. Sauté for 30 seconds.
6. Add bay leaf and canned tomatoes. Stir well.
7. Add red chili powder, turmeric powder, fresh chana masala spice blend, and salt. Cook for 1 to 2 minutes, mixing well.
8. Add soaked, drained chickpeas and 3 cups water, and stir well.
9. Press 'cancel,' close lid, press 'pressure cook,' and set the timer for 35 minutes on high.
10. When Instant Pot beeps, let the pressure release naturally.
11. When pin drops down, open lid. Press 'sauté' mode again and add amchur powder, kasuri methi, and brown sugar.
12. Mash some of the beans with a potato masher and continue to stir well.

13. Let mixture come to a boil, then let simmer for 1 minute.
14. Press 'cancel' and garnish with cilantro (optional).
15. Instant Pot chana masala is ready! Serve hot with roti, poori, or steamed rice.

ALOO MATAR

INGREDIENTS

1 teaspoon cumin seed
1 teaspoon ginger, chopped
1 teaspoon garlic, chopped
1 medium-sized onion, chopped
2 tomatoes, chopped or 2 cups
    canned diced tomatoes
4 red potatoes, cubed
1 cup frozen peas
1 teaspoon red chili powder
¼ teaspoon turmeric powder
½ teaspoon garam masala
salt
2 cups water
1 bay leaf
cilantro for garnish (optional)
½ teaspoon lemon juice

INSTRUCTIONS

1. Press 'sauté' and add oil to inner pot.
2. As oil heats up, add cumin seeds. Sauté them until they start to sizzle.
3. Add garlic, ginger, and chopped onions. Sauté for 2 minutes.
4. Add the chopped tomatoes and spices. Sauté for 2 minutes.
5. Add green peas, potatoes, salt, and water. Stir and close lid.
6. 'Pressure cook' on high for 3 minutes. Wait for 'natural pressure release' (NPR). Wait for silver button to drop before opening lid.
7. Add a splash of lemon juice and sprinkle garam masala on top.
8. Garnish with cilantro (if desired) and aloo matar is ready!
9. Serve hot, paired with steamed rice or roti.

BLACK-EYED PEAS CURRY

 **Prep time: 10 min**

 **Cook time: 20 min**

 **Serves: 5**

INGREDIENTS

1 ½ cups black-eyed peas
2 cups water
1 onion, chopped
2 tomatoes, chopped
¼ inch ginger, chopped
2 garlic cloves, chopped
1 teaspoon cumin seed
½ teaspoon fresh coriander powder
½ teaspoon fresh cumin powder
¼ teaspoon turmeric powder
½ teaspoon red chili powder
2 teaspoons oil
¼ teaspoon garam masala to sprinkle (optional)
cilantro for garnish (optional)

INSTRUCTIONS

1. Soak black-eyed peas for 30 minutes in warm water.
2. Press 'sauté' mode and add 2 teaspoons of oil.
3. As the oil heats up, add cumin seeds. When it starts to crackle, add minced garlic cloves and chopped ginger.
4. Add chopped onion. Sauté for 40 seconds. Continue to stir.
5. Add chopped tomatoes. Sauté for 2 minutes.
6. Add all the spices (coriander powder, cumin powder, turmeric, garam masala, and red chili powder) and continue to stir well for about 20 seconds.
7. Add rinsed black-eyed peas, salt, and water. Stir well.
8. Press 'cancel,' close lid, and turn valve from 'venting' to 'sealing.'
9. Set to 'manual/pressure cook' on high, and set the timer to 12 minutes.
10. Wait for 'natural pressure release' (NPR) when silver button on lid drops.
11. Add garam masala powder and cilantro (if desired). Mix well.
12. Black-eyed peas curry is ready. Serve hot, paired with naan, roti, or rice.

BLACK-EYED PEAS CURRY | PAGE 104

PAGE 103 | ALOO MATAR

PALAK TOFU

 **Prep time: 6 min**    **Cook time: 19 min**    **Serves: 4**

INGREDIENTS

4 cups fresh spinach leaves, chopped

3 green chilies, chopped (not spicy)

14 ounces firm tofu, cubed

1 tablespoon olive oil

½ teaspoon cumin seeds

¾ cup onion, chopped

¾ cup tomatoes, chopped or 1 tablespoon tomato paste

2 garlic cloves, chopped

1 teaspoon ginger, minced

¼ teaspoon green cardamom powder

1 inch cinnamon stick or ¼ teaspoon powder

salt to taste

1 teaspoon coriander powder

½ teaspoon garam masala

¼ to ½ cup water

¼ cup full fat coconut milk (only top fat layer)

INSTRUCTIONS

1. Fry tofu in a non-stick pan with one teaspoon of oil (optional).
2. Press 'sauté' mode and heat 1 tablespoon of oil.
3. Add cumin seeds, and as they start to splutter, add ginger, garlic, red chili, and onions. Sauté for about 2 minutes until onions turn translucent.
4. Add the chopped tomato or tomato paste, green chilies, and spices, and sauté for another 2 minutes.
5. Add water to deglaze the inner pot. Add spinach.
6. Press 'cancel,' and close lid with the vent in sealing position. Set on 'manual/pressure cook' mode for 2 minutes.
7. Once the Instant Pot beeps, let the pressure release naturally for 5 minutes, then manually release the pressure.
8. Blend spinach and other ingredients in the pot to a creamy texture using a hand blender.
9. Add fried tofu, 'press sauté' on low mode, and cook for 1 minute. (You can add non-fried firm tofu too.)
10. Garnish with coconut cream, and you are done! Palak tofu can be served with rice, naan, roti, or paratha.

RAJMA MASALA

Rajma Masala is a popular north Indian cuisine dish. It's prepared by simmering kidney beans in an onion-tomato-based sauce with a few aromatic Indian spices, to get a thick, stew-like consistency.

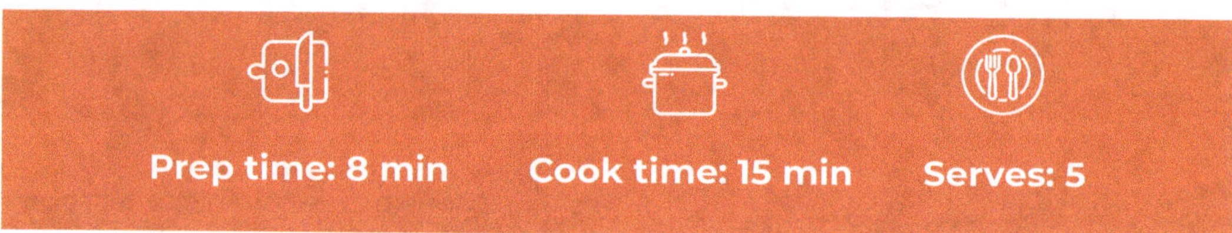

INGREDIENTS

2 cans of red kidney beans or use 1 cup dry kidney beans
1 large red onion, chopped
2 tomatoes, chopped or use ½ cup canned tomatoes
2 teaspoon ginger, grated
2 garlic cloves, chopped
1 teaspoon cumin seeds
1 bay leaf
½ teaspoon red chili powder
½ teaspoon garam masala powder
1 teaspoon coriander powder
¼ teaspoon turmeric powder
¼ teaspoon kasuri methi
Cilantro for garnish
¼ teaspoon amchur powder or use 1 teaspoon lemon juice
1 ½ cups water

INSTRUCTIONS

1. Turn on the Instant Pot and press 'sauté' mode. Heat 1 tablespoon vegetable oil and as the oil heats up, add the cumin seeds and bay leaf. Sauté until the seeds start to sizzle.
2. Add the chopped onions and cook for 3 minutes, until the onion turns slightly soft.
3. Add minced ginger and garlic and cook for 30 seconds.
4. Now add the diced tomatoes and continue to cook until the tomatoes turn soft and mushy (about 3 minutes).
5. Add all the spices and cook for another 2 minutes.
6. Add the canned kidney beans, kasuri methi, and 1 ½ cups of water. Give it a mix and cancel the 'saute' mode. (If you are adding soaked dry beans instead of canned beans, add water until it covers the beans.)
7. Close the Instant Pot lid and turn the vent to the 'sealing' position.

8. Press the 'manual' or 'pressure cooker' mode and cook the rajma for 6 minutes (for soaked beans 30 minutes) on high pressure.
9. Once the Instant Pot beeps, let the pressure release naturally.
10. After the pressure has subsided, stir the curry well and add lemon juice, cilantro, and a little bit of water to get the thickness you prefer.
11. You can also mash some of the beans to make it thicker, but keep in mind that the curry thickens as it cools.
12. Instant Pot kidney beans masala is ready! Serve it hot paired with steamed rice, naan, or bread.

ALOO PALAK

A nutritious, vegan, gluten-free, and mess-free Aloo Palak curry for a weekday; that's such a great gift for a weekday!

INGREDIENTS

1 bunch spinach (palak), chopped

2 garlic cloves, chopped

15 baby potatoes or 2 russet potatoes, cubed

½ inch ginger, grated

1 small onion, chopped

2 tomatoes, chopped or 3 teaspoons tomato paste

½ cup cashews, chopped (optional)

2 green chilies, chopped or ½ teaspoon red chili powder

1 bay leaf

4 cloves, whole

½ inch cinnamon stick

¼ teaspoon turmeric powder

1 teaspoon cumin powder

1 teaspoon coriander powder

1 ½ teaspoons salt

½ teaspoon red chili powder

¼ teaspoon garam masala powder

¼ cup chopped cilantro

¼ teaspoon kasuri methi (fenugreek leaves)

2 teaspoons olive oil

½ teaspoon cumin seeds

INSTRUCTIONS

1. Blend the washed spinach with ½ cup warm water and bring it to a puree consistency. Place it aside.

2. Start the Instant Pot in 'sauté' mode and drizzle a couple of teaspoons of oil. As the oil heats up, add the cinnamon sticks, bay leaf, and cloves. Add the garlic and onions, and saute for 2 minutes.

3. Stir tomato paste, salt, and spices (turmeric, coriander powder, cumin powder, chili powder) with 2 tablespoons water and stir them well.

4. Add cubed potatoes and the blended spinach mixture. Stir well.

5. Press 'cancel' and close the lid with the vent in 'sealing' position. Change the Instant Pot

setting to 'manual' or 'pressure cook' mode at high pressure for 4 minutes.

6. When the Instant Pot beeps, let the pressure release naturally.

7. Prepare tempering by heating one teaspoon oil in a pan and sautéing half teaspoon cumin seeds and a pinch of asafoetida.

8. Once the seeds start to crackle, add ¼ teaspoon of red chili powder and ¼ teaspoon of kasuri methi.

9. Add the tempered cumin seeds and kasuri methi to the dish and give it a good stir. Garnish with cilantro and that's it! Serve it hot with steamed rice or roti.

MUSHROOM CURRY

A creamy, flavorful, and easy mushroom curry for chapati or rice can be a sumptuous dinner option for a weekend or anytime you are entertaining guests outdoors.

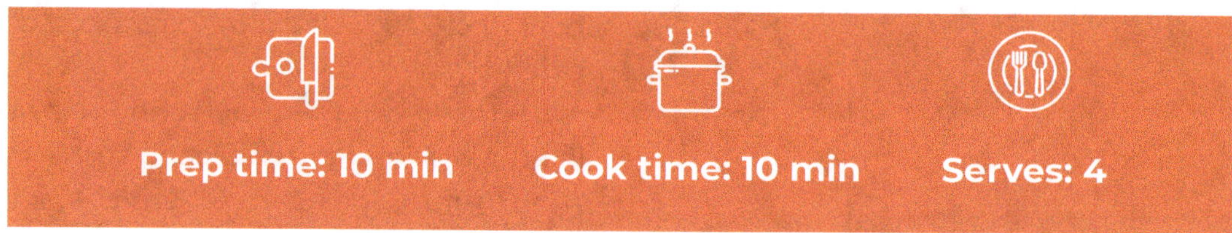

INGREDIENTS

16 ounces mushrooms, sliced

⅓ cup frozen peas

One 15 ounce can diced tomatoes or use 2 tomatoes, chopped plus ½ cup water

1 onion, chopped

1 garlic clove, chopped

½ cup of coconut milk

½ teaspoon garam masala

½ - 1 teaspoon red chili powder

¼ teaspoon turmeric powder

¼- ½ teaspoon cumin powder

Salt to taste

1- 2 tablespoons olive oil

½ teaspoon kasuri methi

Cilantro for garnish

INSTRUCTIONS

1. Start with preparing the sauce by blending canned tomatoes, chopped onions, and garlic.
2. Press the 'sauté' mode and add a couple of teaspoons of oil.
3. When the oil heats up, add the sauce and cook for 2 minutes.
4. Then add red chili powder, turmeric, garam masala, and cumin powder. Stir well and continue to sauté for another minute.
5. Add the sliced mushrooms and frozen peas and continue to stir and cook.
6. Press 'cancel' to stop sautéing and close the lid.
7. Press the 'pressure cook' setting and set the timer for 4 minutes at 'high pressure.'
8. After the time expires, do a 'natural pressure release.' Remove the lid and add coconut milk and kasuri methi.

9. Press the 'sauté' button again and cook for another minute.
10. Garnish with cilantro, and mushroom curry is ready! Serve it hot paired with steamed rice or curry.

ALOO MASALA

Potato Masala, a.k.a Aloo Masala, is one dish that will amaze you with its simplicity, aroma, and taste.

INGREDIENTS

4 russet potatoes, cubed

2 teaspoons cooking oil

1 onion, chopped

1 green chili, chopped

3 teaspoons ginger, grated

1 teaspoon mustard seeds

1 teaspoon urad dal - split black gram

¼ teaspoon turmeric powder

1 strand curry leaves (optional)

1 teaspoon salt

2 tablespoons cilantro, chopped (optional)

INSTRUCTIONS

1. Press the 'sauté' button. Add oil, then when oil is hot, add the mustard seeds and urad dal and let them sputter.

2. Then add the onion, ginger, green chili, turmeric powder, and curry leaves (optional). Stir and cook for 2 to 3 minutes until the onions soften.

3. Add water and deglaze the pot. There should be no browned bits stuck at the bottom of the pot.

4. Add the diced potatoes and salt. Stir and close the lid.

5. Press the 'manual' or 'pressure cook' button and cook on high pressure for 5 minutes, with the pressure valve in the sealing position. After the 5 minutes, quick release the pressure.

6. Open the lid and you may mash the potatoes if you like. I only mashed half the potatoes. (If there is more water it will absorb when you mash the potatoes.)

7. Add the cilantro and mix. If there's any excess water, you can press 'sauté' and stir for a few minutes.

8. Serve potato masala with dosa, poori, and paratha or with rice and dal.

VEGAN DUM ALOO

Vegan Dum Aloo is a flavorful concoction of onion and tomatoes seared in spices and a rich base of cashew paste.

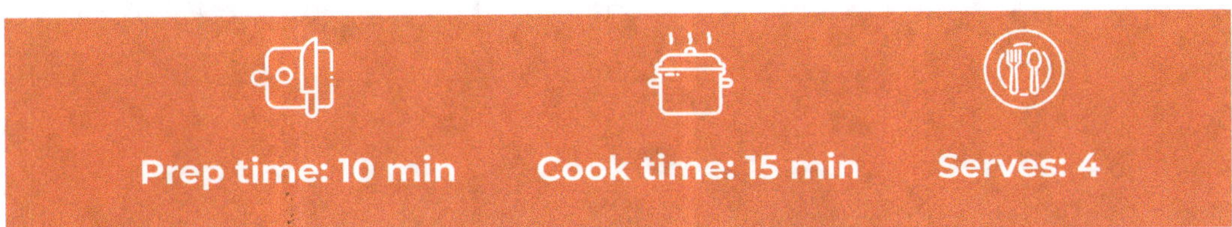

INGREDIENTS

12 -15 baby potatoes, whole and peeled
1 medium-sized onion, chopped
2 small tomatoes, chopped
1 bay leaf
2 green cardamom, whole
4 cloves, whole
2 garlic cloves, chopped
2 teaspoons ginger, minced
2 - 3 tablespoons cashew paste or 20 cashews, whole
2 - 3 tablespoons vegan yogurt
1 ½ teaspoons salt
2 tablespoons cilantro for garnish, chopped or use ¼ teaspoon dry methi leaves
1 teaspoon garam masala
¼ teaspoon turmeric powder
1 teaspoon red chili powder

INSTRUCTIONS

1. Peel the skin of baby potatoes and wash with clean water.
2. Add 2 teaspoons oil to inner pot and press 'sauté' mode.
3. As the oil heats up, sauté bay leaves, green cardamom, cloves, and green chilies.
4. Add minced garlic and ginger, sauté them until they turn golden brown.
5. Meanwhile, blend onions, tomatoes, and cashew paste. If you are using soaked cashews instead of cashew paste, blend them with the tomatoes now.
6. Add the onion-tomato paste to the inner pot and stir well.
7. Add all the remaining spices (turmeric, garam masala, and red chili powder). Cook for 2 minutes.
8. Add salt, vegan yogurt, and potatoes. Stir well.
9. Add a cup of water and close lid.
10. Turn the steam release handle to 'sealing' position, tap 'manual,' and set the timer for 5 minutes.

11. When the time is up, open the lid using 'natural release.'

12. Garnish with dry methi leaves and 2 tablespoons coconut cream (optional).

13. Vegan dum aloo is ready for the table! Serve it hot paired with a cup of steamed rice or chapati!

Vegan Indian Desserts

Desserts are always a fan-favorite, no matter what time of year it is. I love my desserts to be quick and easy so that I can enjoy them with my family. Here are some of the most popular Indian desserts, modified for the Instant Pot. They are all vegan and absolutely delicious!

SABUDANA KHEER

Prep Time: 10 min   Cook Time: 20 min   Soak Time: 10 min   Serves: 4

INGREDIENTS

1 cup sabudana - tapioca pearl
1 ½ - 2 cups water
1 can coconut milk
¼ cup sugar
½ cup jaggery
2 tablespoons cashews,
   chopped
½ teaspoon cardamom powder
3 - 4 saffron strands
pinch of salt

INSTRUCTIONS

1. Soak the clean and rinsed sabudana for 10 minutes.
2. Drain well and put inside the Instant Pot. Add 2 cups of water. Cook for 10 minutes under high pressure (manual mode).
3. Use 'natural release' to let them cook, then open lid.
4. Press 'sauté' setting, and add 1 can of coconut milk, 2 tablespoons cashews, ½ cup of jaggery, and 4 saffron strands. Stir well.
5. Add a few more teaspoons of sugar if you prefer it sweeter.
6. After 2 minutes of boiling, add cardamom powder and switch the Instant Pot off.
7. Let it cool a little, then sabudana kheer is ready! Serve hot or chilled.

CHANA DAL HALWA

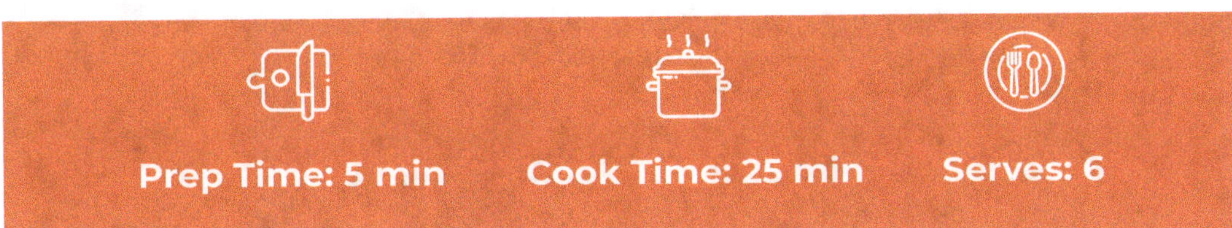

INGREDIENTS

1 cup split Bengal gram/chana
dal

1 cup jaggery

½ cup organic sugar

2 tablespoons corn/avocado oil

15 medium-sized cashews,
chopped

1 cup roasted coconut,
shredded

4 - 6 cloves (spice)

2 tablespoons almond flour
(optional)

INSTRUCTIONS

1. Rinse the Bengal gram or chana dal in clean water 3 times.
2. Cook with 2 cups of water on high pressure for 10 minutes. Check to make sure pressure valve is in 'sealing' position.
3. At the end of 10 minutes, let the pressure release naturally.
4. Open lid, press 'sauté' mode, add jaggery, and mix well.
5. Sauté for 5 to 7 minutes and when it starts to thicken, add crushed cardamoms and cloves, and stir well.
6. Add 2 tablespoons oil, and continue to sauté for 2 minutes with continuous stirring.
7. Add roasted coconuts and cashews. Stir well.
8. When you get the desired consistency, press 'cancel,' and your delicious chana dal halwa is ready to be served.

BADAM BURFI

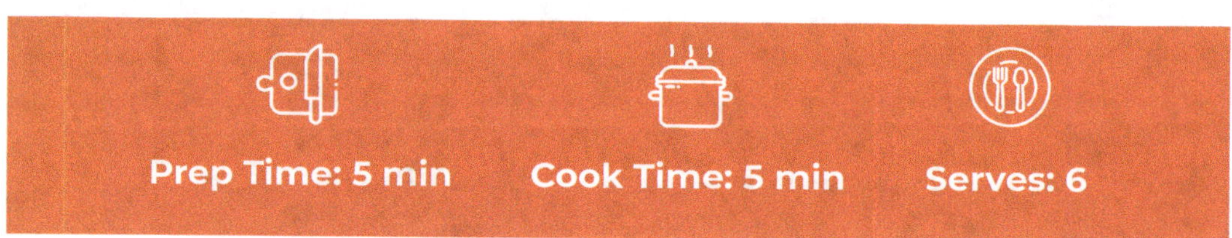

INGREDIENTS

1 cup almond flour, superfine
  blanched
½ cup organic sugar
3 to 4 tablespoons water
1 tablespoon vegan butter or oil
3 to 4 saffron strands

INSTRUCTIONS

1. Add sugar, vegan butter, saffron strands, and water in the inner pot, and mix it well.
2. Close lid, and change the vent setting to 'sealing' mode.
3. Set for 'manual/pressure cook' for 5 minutes.
4. When the pressure cooking cycle is complete, use the 'QR' (quick-release) option.
5. Add 1 cup of almond flour to the sugar syrup, and mix it well to avoid lumps.
6. Grease aluminum foil with vegan butter/oil, and transfer dough to it. Cover with a second greased aluminum foil.
7. Roll dough to your desired thickness.
8. Cut into bite-sized pieces or any desired shape! Enjoy the goodness of almond katli/ badam burfi!

RICE PUDDING WITH MANGO

Prep Time: 5 min **Cook Time: 15 min** **Serves: 5**

INGREDIENTS

1 cup jasmine rice

1 cup almond milk

½ cup of sugar

1 can coconut milk, 13.66 ounces (403ml)

1 ½ cups water

pinch of salt

4 to 5 strands saffron (optional)

¼ teaspoon cardamom powder (optional)

2 ½ cups mangoes, cubed (3 mangoes)

INSTRUCTIONS

1. Make sure that the lid and the sealing ring of the Instant Pot are completely clean and dry with no residues.
2. Add all the ingredients to inner pot, with the exception of chopped mangoes.
3. Stir well, and press 'pressure cook' button. Set timer to 5 minutes, and make sure that the pressure valve is in the 'sealing' position.
4. At the end of 5 minutes, let the pressure release naturally. The pudding will continue to thicken as it cools down.
5. Add a little more milk to get your preferred consistency.
6. Add chopped mangoes. Serve rice pudding warm or cold.

CARROT HALWA

Prep Time: 10 min

Cook Time: 30 min

Serves: 4

INGREDIENTS

4 ½ cups carrot, grated

½ cup sugar

¾ cup almond flour (almond meal)

3 tablespoons avocado oil or olive oil

3 tablespoons roasted cashews, chopped

¼ cup water

½ cup unsweetened plain almond milk

½ teaspoon cardamom powder

INSTRUCTIONS

1. Press 'sauté' and add 2 teaspoons of oil to the inner pot. When oil starts to heat up, add grated carrots, and sauté for 1 minute.
2. Add almond milk and water. Secure lid, close the pressure valve, and cook for 2 minutes on high.
3. Open the valve to quickly release any remaining pressure.
4. Press 'sauté,' and add sugar. Stir for 6 to 7 minutes, or until most of the liquid has reduced.
5. Add remaining oil and almond flour/meal, stir fry the carrots for another 6 minutes, or until they become dry and the oil separates from the mixture. The carrots should look dark orange/reddish in color.
6. Add the cardamom, mix well, and then garnish with chopped nuts (if desired).
7. Serve warm or chilled. If you are making this for a dinner party, serve a small portion of halwa with one scoop of vegan vanilla ice cream.

BUTTERNUT SQUASH HALWA

This is one simple and delicious halwa that is easy to make and tastes great. Try this Instant Pot vegan version of butternut squash halwa!

INGREDIENTS

1 butternut squash, whole

½ cup +1 tablespoon organic sugar

2 tablespoons vegan butter or olive oil

1 teaspoon cardamom powder

2 tablespoons cashews, chopped

1 tablespoon almond flour (optional)

INSTRUCTIONS

1. To prepare the squash, add 2 cups water into the steel inner pot and place a trivet in it.
2. Place the halved, cleaned, and deseeded butternut squash in the trivet.
3. Secure the lid and change the vent setting to sealing mode. Set to 'manual/pressure cook' for 15 minutes.
4. At the end of the time, use the quick release option after 5 minutes to relieve the pressure.
5. Remove the squash and set it aside to cool.
6. Drain any remaining water from the inner pot.
7. Press the 'sauté' button, and add 2 tablespoons vegan butter and the butternut squash after peeling the skin off of it.
8. Mash lightly with a spoon and add sugar and cardamom.
9. Stir-fry for 6 minutes, or until the mixture turns a little darker or when the butter or oil releases a nutty aroma.
10. Garnish with roasted cashew nuts and butternut squash halwa is ready! It is best served as a warm dessert.

VERMICELLI KHEER

Vermicelli kheer is a delicious dessert typically prepared with milk, sugar, and vermicelli strands. This is a simple and delicious Indian dessert.

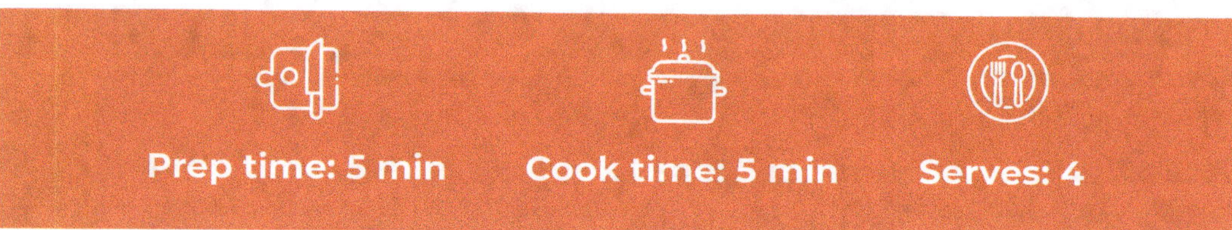

INGREDIENTS

1 cup roasted vermicelli

5 cups almond milk

1 cup water

1 cup sugar

2 green cardamoms, crushed

¼ teaspoon saffron

3 tablespoons cashews, chopped

INSTRUCTIONS

1. Before you begin, make sure that the lid and the sealing ring of the Instant Pot are completely clean and dry. They should have no residue on them.
2. Add all the ingredients one by one to the inner steel pot.
3. Stir and close the pot with the lid. Press the 'porridge' button and set the time to 6 minutes. The pre-set time for porridge mode is 20 minutes, so you have to adjust it down to 6 minutes.
4. Check to make sure that the pressure valve is in the 'sealing' position.
5. At the end of 6 minutes, let the pressure release naturally.
6. The kheer will continue to thicken as it cools down. You might need to add more milk if it thickens more than your preference.
7. Garnish seviyan kheer with chopped nuts or dry edible rose petals and serve warm or cold.

ACKNOWLEDGMENTS

A heartfelt thank you to . . .

God for giving me the courage to write a book that helps me spread the joy of preparing a sumptuous meal!

My husband, Srinivas, who has always stood by me and has supported me throughout this journey.

My two daughters, who always make me feel like I am the best cook in the world.

My extended family, especially my brother-in-law and my nephew, who has always supported me and helped me push my boundaries.

My parents, for always blessing me and believing in me.

All my friends, family, and blog readers for your continuous encouragement and support.

RECIPE INDEX

TOMATO SOUP	45
VEGAN DUM ALOO	115
VEGETABLE BIRYANI	58
VEGETABLE KURMA	98
VEGETABLE PULAO	61
VEGETABLE QUINOA	70
VEGETABLE RICE	53
VERMICELLI KHEER	126